PENGUIN BOOKS

FAR FROM MY HOSPITAL BED: REFLECTIONS ON THE PANDEMIC AND SOCIETY

Dr Teresita Cruz-del Rosario was formerly Visiting Associate Professor at the New York University in Abu Dhabi and also at the Lee Kuan Yew School of Public Policy at the National University of Singapore. She is currently affiliated with the Asia Research Institute at the National University of Singapore where she is a research associate.

She has a background in Sociology, Social Anthropology and Public Administration from Boston College, New York University, Harvard Kennedy School and Harvard University Faculty of Arts and Sciences.

T0001552

Far From My Hospital Bed

Reflections on the Pandemic and Society

Teresita Cruz Del Rosario

PENGUIN BOOKS

An imprint of Penguin Random House

PENGUIN BOOKS

USA | Canada | UK | Ireland | Australia
New Zealand | India | South Africa | China | Southeast Asia

Penguin Books is part of the Penguin Random House group of companies
whose addresses can be found at global.penguinrandomhouse.com

Published by Penguin Random House SEA Pte Ltd
9, Changi South Street 3, Level 08-01,
Singapore 486361

First published in Penguin Books by Penguin Random House SEA 2022

ISBN 9789814954457

Typeset in Garamond by MAP Systems, Bangalore, India

www.penguin.sg

To James, for your constancy

Loss, mourning, the longing for memory, the desire to enter into the world around you and having no idea how to do it, the fear of observing too coldly or too distractedly or too raggedly, the rage of cowardice, the insight that is always arriving late, as defiant hindsight, a sense of the utter uselessness of writing anything and yet the burning desire to write something, are the stopping places along the way. At the end of the voyage, if you are lucky, you catch a glimpse of a lighthouse, and you are grateful. Life, after all, is bountiful.

—Ruth Behar
The Vulnerable Observer: Anthropology That Breaks Your Heart

Contents

Introduction

The idea for this book began in May 2020, just a few months into the pandemic. Then, there were approximately 2 million known infections. As I wrote this in December 2021, the global count had risen to nearly 220 million, all within the span of two years. Reported deaths stood at 5.2 million. In late November 2021, *The Economist* estimated between 10.9 and 20.3 million as the 'true value' and credited the discrepancy to people who have died while infected with COVID but were never tested, and therefore did not enter the official totals. The magazine referred to them as 'excess deaths'.

Having been infected over a year ago, I struggled with fear and anxiety when little was known about the virus. We all knew that it could very quickly cause your airways to contract, leaving little else for your lungs but to struggle with oxygen intake and perhaps expire. Unless you were intubated and isolated in negative air-pressure rooms. Or if your immune system fought off the virus, which mine did, thanks to the excellent medical system of Singapore that spared no expense in making sure all of us who were infected, received the best possible treatment regardless of cost.

In countless ways, this book is very much like COVID-19. There isn't a unifying thesis to string the different chapters together like an academic book. There are no concepts culled from existing literature, nor are there debates that serve as background to the research problem. There is no research design, no null hypothesis, and no models with discrete variables that constitute the explanation and the explanandum. There isn't a methodology to justify the choice and treatment of data, no analytical framework to analyse, explain and predict the phenomenon under study.

Who can explain and predict COVID-19 comprehensively anyway? Two years later, just as the world cautiously reopened, the Omicron variant appeared literally out of nowhere and then spread almost everywhere. In late December 2021, Omicron was detected in about seven countries which sent the global economy into a tailspin and had countries swiftly imposing border restrictions. WHO described it as a variant of 'very high risk' that could lead to surges with 'severe consequences'. In the words of WHO director-general Tedros Adhanom Ghebreyesus,

> . . . many of us think we are done with COVID-19. It's not done with us.

At best, there has been progress in studying the virus's behaviour, how it mutates, lodges itself and ravages the human body, its increasing mutants and variants, and its many after-effects. And still, more studies are ongoing on how the body has been 'de-familiarized' with those who suffer from what has become known as long COVID. The lament is the same for many sufferers: the body is not what it once was. Each day is a struggle to befriend one's body as the after-effects continue to unravel and make themselves felt long after the onset of illness.

Like me. It's been a year of gasping, whether it's ten steps to the kitchen, a flight of stairs, or a gentle morning walk that I struggle with as a matter of reintroducing a pre-pandemic routine. A multitude of online support groups list after-effects, ranging from massive hair loss to debilitating headaches, facial pain and a busted digestive system.

On the unusual bright side, some did report heightened sexual urges. There's a whole chapter devoted to sex and the virus in this book. I enjoyed the research. It taught me about human imagination, especially when carnal desires are at stake. We are an intelligent species, but we are also horny. That's the one urge I daresay that can't be contained.

In the course of two years, we adjusted, resilient humans as we are, despite our resistance to change our habits. For starters, as we all became more familiar with the coronavirus phenomenon, our language did adjust as well. We tamed the virus through COVID-speak. Thus, we learned the first two essential verbs: quarantine and intubate. Once considered the province of medical experts, these two verbs were quickly appropriated and became part of our daily conversation. If you were intubated, you were definitely in mortal danger, even if you could survive the experience as many did. In the presence of an outsider, one's thoughts quickly darted to the quarantine requirements and whether the interloper has fulfilled the mandatory fourteen days of isolation. Other terms followed suit: protocol, antigen, asymptomatic, contact tracing, aerosols, herd immunity, N95 respirator, personal protective equipment (PPE), social distancing, polymerase-chain-reaction test (PCR), flattening the curve. The list goes on, at least five Google pages of coronavirus glossary. The medical lingo became layperson-speak. After a year of this tiresome virus, our vocabulary expanded—something to say for small mercies.

At an astounding speed, several vaccines were produced, tested and released before the end of 2020 to arrest the rate of transmission, to fortify our human bodies against further assault, to lessen the pain of sickness and strengthen our defences in case of another attack. However, the most-anticipated event, except perhaps for the US elections, was the first-ever jab given to Margaret Keenan, a grandmother in the UK, about to turn ninety-one years old. She hailed it as the 'best early birthday present'.

Now, at the one-year mark after the first vaccines were rolled-out, ready for an anxious global population, over eight billion doses have been dispensed. It is uplifting to know that Bhutan has inoculated 94 per cent of its adult population at a record-breaking speed of nine days since it started its vaccination drive in late July 2021. As of December 2021, Bhutan has recorded 957 infections in a total population of 770,000 people. Thus far, only one has died. During the same period, the United Arab Emirates has likewise achieved a 90 per cent vaccination rate of their populations, while Cuba, Chile and Singapore have reached the 85 per cent full vaccination mark.

At the other extreme are several countries that have vaccinated less than 1 per cent of their population: Burkina Faso, Burundi, Cameroon and the Democratic Republic of Congo. While some nations are awash with vaccine supplies, others struggle to receive their share. The United Kingdom, for example, has managed to secure 367 million doses while the European Union has signed contracts for 2.3 billion doses. According to *Politico.com*, if all these contracts materialize, Western Europeans could vaccinate their populations three times over. This pandemic holds up a mirror to humanity—its many imbalances and distortions.

At best, this book echoes the global discombobulation when COVID attacked humanity. The world wrestled with the virus's origins and effects for an entire year, its strains and its mutants. Governments everywhere mounted efforts at prevention, containment, eradication. There was a global response, indeed, but not convincingly everywhere. A few were more successful than others at managing outbreaks. As a result, many countries with significant populations are grappling with successive waves of infection, trying to balance effective health response with economic dislocation.

The outcomes of different countries to contain the outbreak are very much like this book: it attempts to portray a coherent narrative but doesn't, because it can't. So instead, we are all suspended in between muddling-through strategies and rational applications based on limited and still-evolving knowledge as the situation unfolds.

The filmmaker Rodrigo Garcia caught my attention while I was in the hospital over a year ago. He wrote to his famous deceased father, Gabriel Garcia Marquez, whom he endearingly calls Gabo:

> The fog was too heavy . . . I am still unable to frame it all in any satisfying way, to metabolize the shared experience, [whether] as a song, a poem, a movie, or a novel [that] will finally point me in the direction of where my thoughts and feelings about this whole thing are buried.

His letter reminded me of my robust and arrogant thirties when I read his father's novel *Love in the Time of Cholera*. Back then, I was more enthralled with the lovesick Florentino Ariza for Fermina Daza, whom he loved, confounded and unrequited, for 'fifty-one years, nine months and four days'. The gifted novelist compared the pain of such love to the deadly plague of cholera. In my hospital bed, long days and nights waiting for two negative nose-swab results gave me pause on the meaning of life with pain and longing, loneliness and fear, of sorrow and separation from my loved ones, like our hero Florentino in the novel, lovesick for recovery and a return to health.

Thus this book. To help lift this fog. To find sparks of sunlight piercing through and find a clearing somewhere while the mist thickens. As in Marquez's novel, I hope to see redemption for his lovesickness when finally, he conquers Fermina's heart after a long wait of five decades. When finally, humanity prevails over this virus and ends this pandemic. Hopefully not fifty years later.

But this book is not just about me. Instead, this is about all of us, the human species, the changes we've encountered and endured since the stealthy appearance of the coronavirus in late 2019. This book is about the ways we live, love and work. The ways we propagate, reproduce and protect ourselves and each other to ensure that we survive and flourish.

Like Ronald, my friend of over thirty years. The coronavirus has brought us closer digitally. He turned into a gardener, and I watched his transformation, albeit electronically, into a lover of Nature. A chapter on gardening highlights Ronald's expansion as a human being, as his sights have been reset and his hands follow his vision of weaving urban concrete into green landscapes. This is a joyful moment to detect and uncover those mysterious spaces that enlarge us as a species. In that respect, I hope the pandemic forces us to rebuild this environment with more thoughtful consideration.

Because I have a historical-sociological view of human life, I write about the societies we've built and the civilizations we've left behind that testify to our endurance and magnificence. The monuments that have been erected in many our name, some of them submerged by time and destruction, some of them re-emerging so that we may understand our human forebears—how they too lived and loved and worked—so that our species can expand and magnify. Frank Snowden's recent book on *Epidemics and Society* is an elaborate reminder of how pandemics reflect and shape human societies throughout the ages. In countless ways, the pandemic behaviours of the present echo those of the past and how history is a mirroring of all that humans have done and continue to do. Looking back at who we were, perhaps, we might be guided today to who we might still become. Maybe come to know, as well, the pandemics that devastated human civilizations throughout history and the utter frailty of many of our pursuits.

This book is also about our very many follies. We continue to commit a kind of time-release suicide. We create environments that choke us and demolish landscapes that sustain us. Many commentaries have claimed that the virus thrives in dense environments, facilitating the jump from animals to humans. Alongside other utterly useless creations are the multiple military-defence systems that can obliterate the planet eighty times over. Why would we even need more stockpiles of bombs and missiles when one nuclear bomb could effectively do the job of ending all human life?

This book also touches on our imperfections and the flaws of our species highlighted in the time of COVID. We quarrel and bicker, argue and debate the finest, littlest, insignificant details. We are petty, unkind, distrustful, selfish, ungenerous. We gloat with our minor victories, unmindful that these are fleeting. We are vengeful, self-righteous, hateful. We perceive ourselves in overblown proportions, forgetting that we are but a lit matchstick, burnt in a fraction of a second. So, I have reserved space in this book for writing stories of misbehaviours. Many of them are worldwide, and many of these misdeeds are astounding. Like the one who gave a sexual massage at the height of lockdown in Singapore in April 2020. A bunch of mindless young adults went partying on a yacht in Singapore in late December 2020 and posted the unphysically distanced gathering on Facebook. And still another spat in the face of someone at the cash register. Why do humans misbehave even when it's full public knowledge that such actions endanger others? It's a question I write about, even if I don't pretend to know the answers.

For two years, we could not touch each other, or do air travel. We were homebound. We couldn't share meals, pray together, teach in classrooms, extend our hands, reveal our faces, watch a concert, drop by a friend's home for tea, applaud our graduating son, give a daughter in marriage, witness the birth of a newborn, pamper grandchildren. We couldn't hug each other to say hello and goodbye. I have written a chapter on my mother and her enduring isolation for over two years now. She is bereft of all human interaction. We, her children, are pixels on a screen every Sunday as we Zoom through lunch instead of family gatherings. I try to understand the human emotion of loneliness, knowing that for some, like my sister in Europe, aloneness is a cultivated friendship with the self.

Our faces remain half-hidden. Our hands wrinkle from washing them multiple times a day. We stand far apart. We live far away. To get closer, we Zoom and Skype. I'll Viber you and you WhatsApp me. Apps govern our daily lives on a mobile phone. We teleconnect and teleconfer, even as my 100-year-old mother still won't handle a mobile phone, much less learn to use it. My father who passed away two decades ago got as far as email. So there is still among us a lost generation who can't and won't surrender to the inevitability of virtual existence.

We've invented many material things to connect us across physical distance. And reinvented them, each a better version of the one that preceded it. Our voices and images travel across continents, and we are connected instantly to separated family and friends, seeing them in the kitchen, the study room, the garden. We can even worship in the utmost private spaces through live-streamed religious rituals. We invented technology, tamed it, embraced it. In the time of COVID, our foremost concern is the strength of our bandwidth, to retain the connection to other humans even as we are physically separated from them. There is a chapter on digital worship and the formation of faith communities to bridge the separation. However, s/he may be conceived, God is a central figure in the pandemic story.

COVID hastened our digitalization. Our language evolved into digi-speak. The survivors of the last generation will sit in silence, unable to comprehend and participate in Twitter conversations, stuck to television, refusing to handle the mobile phone or surf YouTube. Whereas each day, our lives are scheduled around Zoom meetings. The choice of webinars across the globe bombard us with digital decisions. I write about our Zoom family reunions, digital marathons actually, where our endurance to stare and speak into a screen is matched by some of the surprising things we discover about each other, now that there is time to sit, talk and watch without heed for time of day and night.

This book looks at many disjunctures and disconnections. Virtually, we are more connected through stronger bandwidths, yet we are isolated and far removed from the next person from whom we are physically distanced. In the time of COVID, human beings were connected separately. In the time of COVID, it's a high-tech low-touch life.

No single human being has been left untouched. Those born in this era will be marked by a life that is nowhere close to those their parents lived, even if they will be nourished and fed by them. A generation reared during the pandemic has already been born. We can even now ponder the gaps between them and their parents as they grow into adulthood, never experiencing the COVID-free world of their forebears.

This book touches on intergenerational relations and their discontinuities, much like the baby boomers of the 1950s who cannot comprehend the traumas of their parents and grandparents who lived through World War I. Likewise, this generation barely recalls the Vietnam War or the wars in Afghanistan and Iraq in the aftermath of 9/11. Indeed, a millennial nephew said the term 'coronnials' has gained traction and has sprouted into the daily vocabulary.

Then there is racism rearing its ugly head once again. There have been far too many instances where Asians the world over have been subjected to abuse and violence as the debate rages about the source of the virus. Was it a bat in a Wuhan wet market or an escaped virus in a research laboratory? As the propaganda battle rages for pinpointing responsibility for this pandemic, the past traumas return when racism was at the forefront of social life. As when Chinese migrants fled to different parts of South East Asia to escape Mao's revolution in 1949, only to be met with discrimination in many countries as they attempted to re-establish their lives. Today, they are the object of the same venom.

Being Asian outside Asia these days is a social drawback. Any Asian is conflated with Chinese; therefore, all Asians are guilty of spreading the virus. The 'yellow peril' has returned. Unless you are a light-skinned Asian, you might be exempted from the charges of complicity.

There is a chapter on racism, a meditation on the long-standing human failure to confront difference and celebrate it, rather than use it to demonize the Other. Racism is, as so many have observed and commented upon, one of the pandemics of this age. COVID has unwittingly unleashed it globally. But so are fights against it. In this respect, the surfacing of old hatreds and prejudices forces a painful conversation now taking place everywhere. In some areas, more intense than in others.

The virus recalls past traumas in numerous ways. My mother fears food shortages, the same ones she endured during World War II in her tender twenties. A colleague who was a student activist in the Philippines in the 1970s recalls the return of martial law as soldiers patrol the streets to enforce lockdowns in Manila. A fellow researcher draws parallels between the pandemic and the traumas of persecution of the Rohingyas in Myanmar. Another refers to the communist purge in Indonesia in 1965, the race riots in Malaysia in 1964, the tsunami in Thailand, Sri Lanka and Indonesia in 2004. In the time of COVID, we refer to the past and recall those moments in our world to understand collective pain, or what the medical anthropologist Arthur Kleimann terms 'social suffering'.

But COVID has also brought out a sterling quality among the human species—that of unimaginable generosity. For example, a twenty-year-old student-cum-entrepreneur named Ray Lee Sheng whose food business collapsed during the lockdown period in

Singapore. Immediately, he converted his stall into a noodle shop to distribute free packed noodles to vulnerable households. His army of volunteers grew over the weeks, including drivers, cooks and chefs who had lost their jobs. As a final touch, a facial mask is attached to every noodle pack, and then the volunteers head out in their cars for the day's distribution. They exceeded their quota of distributing 20,000 food packages for eight weeks and were overwhelmed by the generosity of donations, whether of money, kitchen space, food ingredients or free labour. I wrote a chapter on Ray Lee Sheng, whom I have still to meet, but who fired up my imagination when I read about his philanthropy while I was in the hospital. I wrote to understand what makes people generous. I haven't yet discovered the answer except through scholarly studies by Kristen Renwick Monroe on altruism and William Hamilton's concept of kin altruism. I am still waiting and hoping to meet Ray Lee Sheng, whose business has flourished. He is now every bit a budding entrepreneur, even while he retains his noodle-donating activities to Singapore's elderly.

I thought of the utter dedication of the volunteers who served me my quarantine notice on a Sunday afternoon and their daily calls to check my temperature. I surrendered to the medical experts, including the nose-swabbers who inflicted utmost discomfort with every nose swab. While my body learned to endure physically, I dutifully answered every question from the contact tracers, who patiently put together a profile of all my movements to establish the pattern of my infection. We were going to battle together, all of us in hospitals all over the world, against this monstrous virus before we were devoured by it.

These are the themes and dimensions of this book, explored through the lens of a COVID survivor. These are the thoughts that flitted, fluttered and formed as I battled the virus and experienced life as never before: one of danger, fear and confusion, but also of hope, admiration and trust.

I write in different tones, styles and forms. There are essays and stories, poems interwoven with prose, analyses drawn from expert opinion, pandemic-stricken voices from our everyday world. There are the prominent looming figures of current history, but many more about the untold struggles of everyday undocumented people—their successes, failures, fears and overcomings. Sometimes I write in long-winding circuitous sentences and paragraphs, a hazard of my academic training. At other times, I play with short, staccato-like prose. One word. One-sentence paragraphs. For emphasis, for humour. Finally, or perhaps just at that moment, my thoughts have come to an abrupt end.

Much like this virus. Outbreaks temporarily abate, until another sneak attacks that leave countries struggling to regain control. Nearly all of Europe is battling to contain the latest episode dealt by Omicron. Holland faced an intense lockdown through the Christmas holidays in December 2021, while Israel and Japan have banned all foreign entry.

This book ends with a plea. I invoke the theory of the psychic unity of mankind from the German ethnographer and anthropologist Adolf Bastian—that we humans, despite our bedazzling variety, are one. 'Standing beneath the same sun, we are all equal,' wrote a wise but anonymous essayist in cyberspace. Although we may have shrugged off Bastian's truism as cliché, COVID has brought forward this postulate as the most enduring lesson today. The virus makes no distinction as to race, age, gender, status, or nation. The xenophobes are hard at work to counter the truism, but the virus gives them a run for their mouth and their money. COVID is a story that teaches us to be better humans. We have been given the gift to renew our human world.

The responses to renewal have been varied: there is a global effort to produce and distribute vaccines despite hesitation and resistance; philanthropy and volunteerism are showing themselves at their best. Others profit opportunistically by hoarding precious commodities. A few misbehave. Like that jerk who spat in the masked face of another unsuspecting pedestrian, all his venom spewed publicly for no reason other than that he needed to vent his pent-up resentment. Or the fight at a supermarket over toilet paper.

These were two years of elation and sadness. In May 2020, Susie Orbach, a British writer in the *Guardian*, said COVID is a sad story. Despite its sadness, however, this

> . . . societal trauma gives opportunities for people to go through things together, rather than suffer alone, to find new ways to live with our fears

and discomforts, to overcome COVID-minted social phobias, to find a
way to build bonds of attachment and respect.

We have been thrown together on this assaulted planet at a moment
when we've looked at one another more closely than we ever have.

I remember vividly when I came home after twenty-five days in the
hospital in April 2020. I had kept the taxi receipt of that precious day
as a distinct memory of when I marvelled and gasped at the near-empty
streets of Singapore, save for a solitary cyclist and a vigorous jogger.
Then, I was, and still am, a different person. A bit broken but refusing
to yield. Every day, a battle to put the pieces together and befriend the
new fragments of self. To endure more, to maintain faith, to deepen
my understanding about this troubled world and how we altogether
might restore and renew it.

And yes, I have been vaccinated. It was exact full year since I was
released from the hospital when I received my second dose. It did feel
full circle.

I wake up every day to the thought that I have regained my life, and
hopefully, the fullness of my breath will return. I am hoping to sprint
in the gym again. I swim almost daily and will aim for 8,000 steps, as
was my pre-virus exercise record. Even as I accept that my life remains
precarious, as all our lives have become, we will live on. In these long
two years of confusion and anxiety, we will find, as Gabriel Garcia
Marquez did,

. . . the time (we became) most conscious of and grateful for (our)
incredible victories over adversity.

Singapore
24 December 2021

Chapter 1

Thank You, Doc, For the Crackers[1]

Some dates you don't forget. And some places too.

Like the morning of 9/11 at the Boston College quadrangle where I, along with other students en route to our respective buildings, stood frozen at the news that the World Trade twin towers fell. Instinctively, we all looked up at the empty September sky, unsure of what we hoped to see. It was a full ten minutes before we dared to move again.

Likewise, I remember the shuttle-bus ride vividly in late March a year ago, on the way to the park for a morning walk. Since my husband and I moved to this serviced-apartment complex in Singapore, Raymond, our driver, was a friendly chatterer for two years. He knew all of his passengers that he had served for nearly twenty years. Who came, stayed, visited, left, returned. He tucked the baby strollers in the back, fixed the seating arrangements and scheduled the passengers in the van according to their drop-off points. He knew all the stops of his daily routes, the people he ferried, the laundry pick-up, the mail exchange between two serviced-apartment buildings, the executive

---

1 An original version of this article with the same title appeared in *Today*, an online publication in Singapore on 11 May 2020

staff, the itinerant tenants. He was proud to be a working man still. Over seventy years old, he was strong and healthy, played basketball thrice a week. He reported daily at 5.30 a.m. and ended his driving duties at noon.

A twenty-seater Mercedes Benz van with external silver and purple paint and an orchid logo was its mark of recognition. Always clean and spanking-handsome, leather-upholstered seats and functioning seatbelts, you couldn't miss it on the road. Not when you flagged Raymond. He remembered all of his passengers.

'I pick you up in another hour, this same spot on the other side,' he instructed. 'Waiting time only two minutes.' Every day for two years, no-fail.

Until that morning in late March 2020 when he reported feeling unwell. 'I don't feel good today. So, I go to the clinic after my shift. I think it's my prostate,' he said. Then he waved goodbye. 'See you tomorrow,' and Raymond was off for the day.

That was the last time I saw him. Three days later, Raymond tested positive for COVID.

I went into quarantine on the weekend when the condo estate management informed us of Raymond's positive infection. I came forward to indicate that I was one of the exposed passengers.

The ministry of health officials served my 'quarantine notice' the following day. A temperature monitoring sheet had to be filled out thrice daily. After that, the health ministry would call me to record and report my temperature.

I camped out on the sofa of my study room, sequestered the guest bathroom. Towels were segregated for me. A bottle of disinfectant and alcohol spray stood on a ledge in the bathroom. Lots of handwashing, wiping of doorknobs with disinfectant. Meals were left outside my door. Plates and utensils were set aside for my exclusive use.

I started to feel physical discomfort as my temperature see-sawed above 37°C, but none too alarming. I wasn't battered sick. I played video games, binge-watched Netflix, worked on a policy report, did some writing assignments. And fretted a bit. Something different was taking place in my body.

The health ministry called me on the fifth day of my quarantine. My temperature shot up to 37.8°C. I reported my exposure to Raymond, our shuttle-bus driver, confirmed to have COVID a week ago. A quick check at the other end of the line. In less than half an hour, an ambulance came to fetch me.

I boarded the ambulance to take me to Tan Tock Seng Hospital in Singapore. On the morning of 2 April 2020 at 9.30 a.m., I waved goodbye to my husband. Still wearing my cargo shorts and cotton T-shirt cut at the sleeves, faded leather slip-on shoes, an oversized handbag and a charger for my phone was all I carried. I wasn't prepared for an extended hospital stay. It was a mild fever for five days, nothing more. So, I assumed it would be resolved quickly.

We arrived at the hospital driveway of the National Center for Infectious Diseases (NCID), the only destination for COVID-positive patients in Singapore. All outfitted in yellow PPEs, an army of medical personnel stood at the entrance. An usher walked me into the ground floor, where I took my physically distanced seat to fill out forms. We were four people surrounded by about sixteen medical staff.

An X-ray confirmed that my lower right lung had started pneumonia. A battery of tests ruled out dengue, influenza A and B. Finally, COVID. I tested positive. Right on schedule. Exactly four days since I was exposed.

Two quick journeys. One drop-off, one pick-up. Altogether a twenty-minute ride. COVID didn't need more time. I knew it, felt it. Despite my mental denials, the body never lied. There was something that had lodged into my system. This devious little virus had managed to sneak in.

It was an odd feeling of relief: the guessing game was finally over. And I was in one of the best hospitals in the world. No overcrowding. No long queues of people waiting to be admitted. In less than thirty minutes, I occupied an entire room and bathroom all to myself. Right next to me was a ceiling-to-floor window where sunlight shone through. I had a privileged view of the tree-lined pavement below and the entrance to the emergency landing where I had arrived just a few hours ago.

My infection was none too severe, and I didn't need to be isolated further. I was transferred one floor down to the shared ward the following morning, where we would be two persons to a room. Same room size but with two beds and a shared bathroom. I kept the bed closest to the window. The sunlight streamed in and the trees looked larger from one floor below. A bit more noise too from the streets. Some mornings, two visiting maya birds pecked on the glass window. Lots of electrical sockets, a bell buzzer, an electronic bed with push buttons to raise or lower any part of your body: raise your feet, lower your head, elevate your torso. A flimsy yellow curtain on a railing could be drawn to conceal the patient from view completely. A small, glass-encased cabinet to pick up and drop off food, pyjamas and medicines to minimize human contact. And double sliding doors to keep the indoor room temperature constant. This felt like a five-star COVID hotel.

My first roommate arrived in the early evening with a bad cold and cough and a big appetite for lengthy mobile-phone conversations. She was a medical assistant at the same hospital, eager to leave as quickly as possible. She did go after five days when her viral load lowered and she could wait out the shedding of viral fragments in the recovery facility that Singapore had built quickly in the early days of the pandemic.

Then the battery of tests and doctors' consultations followed. Daily swabs and follow-up X-rays monitor vital stats to check blood pressure, blood count and oxygen levels. Coordinated morning phone calls with my husband for updates. WhatsApp messages galloped across the globe with my scattered siblings in Asia, Europe and the US. They chewed their nails to the quick with each report as my husband sat at home and anchored the global broadcast of my progress. Prayer brigades for my recovery proliferated, and I received digital blessings from unimaginable corners of the world.

On an evening when my fever spiked to 38.5°C, my doctors advised a week-long course of hydroxychloroquine to bring down the fever. Remdesivir was still undergoing trials. The diabolical taste of the tablets lingered on my tongue, and I hungered for watermelons. Otherwise, I cared nothing more than to survive this bitter week of medicines.

I learned soon after that the entire hospital personnel from all medical units and departments were deployed to the NCID. They were all dressed similarly—the doctors and nurses, the medical technicians and the cleaners were like an army arrayed in yellow plastic—steady and perpetual presences, performing their jobs with efficient dedication. Someone would always quietly pick up the garbage from the bathroom at way past midnight. Every single day and night, no fail.

At night, I had a ringside view of the nurses' workstation. They were a red-button-call away. A small sensor pasted on my belly and connected to an outside computer gave them ready access to any changes in my body temperature. They were always prepared to minister to every patient's need at any hour, be it the daily dose of Panadol or a request for milk, tea and biscuits.

On one such morning, two weeks after being hospitalized, I told Dr Eugene, the regular morning doctor who checked my lungs, how hungry I was and that my taste buds were aching for truffle-cheese pizza. My appetite had returned, my symptoms had subsided and I was slowly regaining strength. But we needed to wait for the two consecutive negative swab results before I could be discharged. The following day, he came with two packets of Meiji crackers and a sliver of cheese tucked in a plastic food container.

'Just don't eat the silica gel, even if you're that hungry.' We both laughed. I have been committed to Meiji crackers as my daily afternoon snack ever since.

Beating COVID-19 was indeed more than just a biomedical battle.

In the earliest days of my confinement, I was visited by dark thoughts, felt bleak and despaired often enough to entertain questions of my survivability. I read updates of the spread in other countries. I devoured news stories of other patients who went through similar predicaments, some of them worse than mine. Someone was delirious with a 39°C fever and hallucinated. Whereas I merely suffered from fluctuating fever, occasional asthma attacks, enormous fatigue and lack of strength but none too debilitating. The short walks to the bathroom would tire me, all ten steps of them, and I suffered a loss of appetite for the first two weeks. I read, clung to my hopes, and bravely fought my demons.

Then the battlefield shifted into the arena of prolonged patience, fighting off confinement-induced boredom and tolerating my roommates' idiosyncrasies. One snored until I thought my eardrums would burst; another engaged in mobile-phone marathons until the batteries died, and another devoured cartoons nonstop on the hospital television monitor. Six roommates later, I'd developed a tolerance for sharing small spaces with total strangers whose only commonality with me was a debilitating virus that continued to confound us all. I joked with my husband and siblings that this was the COVID version of speed-dating. My humour was back, I knew I was going to live.

Twenty-five days and eleven nose swabs later, Dr Eugene announced the good news that two consecutive negative swab tests allowed me to return home. He reached out with his blue surgical gloves to squeeze mine, especially happy, proud and honoured. He said that I was his second successful patient from the academe that he had had the privilege to take care of. I asked for his full name and email address, determined to write him of my deep gratitude.

He replied, stating that it was his team, all the others who worked together to treat us, one patient at a time. Then, with characteristic humility and humour, he stated that his only significant role was to provide me with cheese and crackers as a respite from hospital food.

Someday, I thought then, not in the too distant future, I would love to return to the fifth floor of the Tan Tock Seng Hospital, where I passed nearly a month of my life, the most memorable one to date. Indeed, a defining moment when pondering my mortality was so real and immediate. And to meet Dr Eugene, whose face I never saw. A mask always covered him. His eyes were hidden behind thick plastic goggles, his hands were wrapped in blue surgical gloves and a protective, yellow, plastic coat covered his clothes that he would remove after leaving my hospital room when his morning visits to COVID-19 patients ended.

I hoped to meet the nurses and the medical technicians, the sweepers and the cleaners who drew my blood and swabbed my nose oh so many times, wrapped the plastic garbage and quietly slipped out at midnight.

Shake their hands without fear or trepidation. Without yellow PPEs, masks, goggles and gloves. Remember each one of them by name. Speak my gratitude and admiration with no need for a one-metre distance. And all around, rejoice that in this formidable battle still raging, we can celebrate our victory at becoming a better species who fought tooth and nail to care for each other.

I left Tan Tock Seng hospital confident there would be a return visit. A triumphant one.

Well, it did happen. Five months later, in October 2020, Singapore entered Phase 2 with fewer restrictions on mobility and safety measures all in place. Infection rates had gone considerably lower, and the outbreaks in the migrant dormitories were successfully controlled through a strict testing regime and physical distancing. Community infections were close to zero, and confidence returned to the populace.

Dr Eugene and I met at the hospital entrance, where I spent nearly a month half a year ago. Both masked, we headed to a nearby café, got our ritual temperature check, took our seats in a physically distanced café. And then, like a long-awaited moment of truth, we faced each other, sipping herbal tea and biting into black forest cake.

His face, fully unmasked, clean-shaven, with the same warm eyes that gleefully served me crackers and cheese during my three-and-a-half-week confinement.

'Now everyone in the hospital knows I sneaked in the cheese and crackers for you,' he joked.

No goggles this time, no gloves. Our masks were parked on the table. Just food. It was a moment to reflect upon: when humanity reencounters each other after what seemed like an eternity of separation, the first instinct is to eat. A reminder, perhaps, that when life is precarious, one must nourish it.

I launched into his intellectual biography, the researcher that I am and therefore couldn't help myself. I wanted to know what drove him to become a doctor.

'It was SARS in 2003,' he said. It was an inspirational moment for him to dedicate his life to medicine. He volunteered as a temperature screener outside the hospital premises of the National University Hospital, where he was enrolled as a medical student. Okay, it paid him $8 an hour, and for a medical student, the payoff was hot noodles in the hospital canteen and an occasional coffee break at Tea and Leaf café.

He showed me pictures of his two sons, one of whom will celebrate his birthday in ten days. I sent a chocolate mousse. His son thanked me via WhatsApp, a five-year-old cutie who melted my heart on digi-space.

Because of COVID, I gained a friend. This virus was at least good for something.

No longer doing the rounds to check on COVID patients, Dr Eugene resumed his medical duties as a hematology specialist. He published an article in the *Lancet* journal early this year to recognize the role of NGOs in Singapore that ministered to the needs of the migrant workers who made up 90.6 per cent of infection rates. He wanted to make a point:

> ... the humanity, compassion, and generosity toward the less fortunate from a concerned citizenry through NGOs.

The article mentioned many of them: Transient Workers Count Too, Alliance of Guest Workers Outreach, COVID-19 Migrant Support Coalition, Crisis Relief Alliance, Migrant Workers' Centre, ItsRainingRaincoats.

This year had seen the best of humanity because of so many who came out in full force when they were called upon during the outbreak. At the hospital level, several initiatives went into full operation. The Singapore Straits Times reported in April 2020 that swab teams were formed to staff the frontlines during Singapore's critical first five months. Code DORSCON (Disease Outbreak Response System Condition) orange meant the escalation of the severity of the public health situation. Singapore went into the mobilization of its best weapon—its human resources.

Their many voices were compiled and collated in a sort of collective memoir which the Tan Tock Seng Management Development Office published. They all referred to the team experience as the 'kampung spirit', a Malay term for community.

Lua Yan Bin, a management fellow at the Tan Tock Seng Hospital, spoke of a constant review of workflows at the entrance screening. Streamling of patient and visitor flows was necessary to ensure that the hospital intake was not overwhelmed or the staff overburdened. Thus, time segments and corresponding daily shifts optimized staff input and productivity even during the months when infections escalated in Singapore. Any one of them would have met me at the hospital entrance when I arrived for COVID screening a year ago.

Jim Tan, a management associate, learned about swabbing and the associated processes of setting up swab stations, preparing test kits, verifying patient identity and handling completed swab samples. His team also trained nursing-home staff.

Many others spoke of sacrifices, from postponed holidays and weddings to segregation from their families to prevent transmission. There is no discordant voice in a hospital of about 9,000 staff, despite the fear and exhaustion, the multiple tasks and challenges, the breakneck speed of many operations. But above all else, said Benjamin Tan, a management associate,

> . . . the key ingredient was trust—an intangible sense that teammates will get the job done.

At the last sip of our tea during our post-recovery meeting, Dr Eugene offered a parting shot, his best one that I recall:

> Go out with your friends, enjoy your life. Community infections are close to zero.

That was in September 2020, before Delta, before Omicron, before subvariants BA.1, BA.1.1 and BA.2.

I did. Proudly reported to my female colleagues that I am medically cleared to socialize. We ate Greek food with gusto in an open-air restaurant where grilled pieces of lamb and hearty servings of moussaka competed with an expansive view of Singapore's famous Dempsey Hill. We were gluttons for human time together, for the camaraderie that we sorely missed, for offline, real-time friendship. Food was a side event.

But I never saw Raymond again. He has not returned to driving the shuttle bus. It's been nearly two years, and there has been no sight of him, none of the familiar figure strolling by the gardens of the apartment complex in the early morning, waiting for the first wave of passengers. He has recovered and reported to the administration staff, but not much more information. Instead, he disappeared very quietly, as we all do when we become statistical entries in the global process of COVID accounting.

Thank you for the ride, Raymond, wherever you are. Thank you Tan Tock Seng Hospital staff, for the tirelessness and dedication that continue to this day, long after I have left. And thank you, Dr Eugene, for the crackers.

Chapter 2

The Body in Isolation, the Mind in Solitude

Lockdown in the Philippines began on 12 March 2020.

My 100-year old mother, who lives almost totally alone in her three-storey, six-bedroom mansion, created an ecosystem and has maintained it for over two years now.

She remembers the day she received the pronouncement from the government. 'I was saddened (*nalungkot ako*),' she recalled, a clever linguistic device in our language that suggested she was not a sad person at heart but was forced to become sad by the sudden handing down from the central authorities the nationwide order for everyone to stay indoors.

It lasted for nearly three months. Metropolitan Manila of six municipalities, previously bustling with 17 million people hustling about daily in legendary tangled human and vehicular traffic, fell into emptiness.

She lives with a line-up of five household staff, all under a state of almost permanent quarantine. Apart from controlled movements to the supermarket five minutes away outside the gated community, no one has ventured out of my mother's household for two years. Even after lifting the lockdown in late June, she does not dare venture outside. Lately, with the daily spike in coronavirus infections, she has banned travel out of the house and resorted to home deliveries instead. Every item that entered the house was transferred into a separate receptacle right at the gate; their contents were thoroughly washed and disinfected. Everyone hand-washed and body-splashed with Green Cross alcohol before crossing the threshold from the kitchen door into the living room.

Her afternoon Mahjong sessions ceased. The chatter over fast-moving tiles in the air-conditioned anteroom by her bedroom vanished. The competent and able-bodied Grace, the household's maître d', has not cooked heavy afternoon snacks for the Mahjong mates in over a year. She turned to YouTube instead to discover new dishes to experiment with, in the hope that when the virus takes leave, and the cackling matrons return for a six-hour four-way Mahjong battle, she is on the ready with her latest culinary presentation.

One of her Mahjong mates passed away from a lingering illness within that year. Another moved out of Manila into the provinces to escape urban suffocation and enjoy the rural openness. The virus purportedly thrives in dense urban environments.

The rituals of a very long day, bereft of outside human interaction, refocused my mother's attention on daily garden inspection. She ordered the turning of every stone, leaf and stem to detect uninvited insects, unwanted debris, wayward branches and overgrown tendrils that have no place in her otherwise pristinely manicured garden. Are gutters swept clean of fallen leaves, potted plants watered, the small fountain pump checked for blockages? When those questions were satisfactorily answered, the routine turned upstairs to the second and third floors. Check the unused bathrooms, all eight of them. Are the valves closed, water closets dry, bidets turned off? Is there a water leakage unsuspectingly seeping into someone's bedroom? Have rusty showerheads been scrubbed with the steel scourer?

In the early evening, the doors and windows are boarded up. She is deathly afraid of the virus that might float into her home from the neighbour in the house behind hers, a COVID suspect. The elegant, wrought-iron doors that look out into the unused swimming pool are bound together by a heavy chain wrapped around thrice and then padlocked for the night. Any burglary attempt would have been thwarted just by the cacophony of rattling steel.

She finally withdraws into her bedroom to face the evening after a solitary meal, closing behind her three doors, all locked from the inside. Her caregivers gingerly peel off her clothes, slip her into a nightdress, pull up her socks to keep her feet warm, moderate the aircon temperature and switch on the television to a series of telenovelas that would lull her to sleep. One night, it would be the battle for the family inheritance and the secret love child that turned up at the doorstep to claim his rightful share; another evening's script would be a long courtship between lovers that must decide among other equally good-looking competitors for their respective attention. This daily rigamarole would repeat itself as daylight crept across the wood-panelled ceilings of her stylish bedroom, and she began the same long journey of another uneventful day.

Almost at the end of her odyssey in this human world, she is suddenly left with no one; it's just she and her employed household staff. Together they endure, perforce, the long, lonely months of forbidding isolation. Her two sons, living some kilometres away in different municipalities in the metropolis, dared not brave the streets. They might encounter numerous checkpoints manned by the local military to enforce the lockdown. The family doctors advised that her near-perfect ecosystem should remain undisturbed.

When I finally saw my mother after two years in December 2021, she was a mere shadow of herself. Isolation had diminished her physically and mentally. Totally bereft of human communication, her speech became short and halting. She was almost physically immobile. Yet her faculties never faltered, and she gathered her memories of the past into a soliloquy of remembrances. She recreated her world through her treasure trove of bygone decades. It was perhaps her only remaining strategy to endure the prolonged and bitter separation.

Isolation has hit just about every household the world over. Fear of the virus and its rapid spread pushed humanity back inside the cave. Under lockdown, the world narrowed to almost a sliver. There is no one to touch, to hold and to be close to. Interactive space collapsed.

In my Catholic world, the image of Pope Francis was starkly desolate as he delivered the 'Urbi et Orbi (to the City and the World)' prayers at a completely emptied St Peter's Square in late March 2020. The platform on which he stood glistened from the reflected glow of six candelabras amidst the pouring rain. The grey, granite stairs that led up to the platform were a grand emptiness. So stark and maybe even aesthetically beautiful as dark stone and golden light illuminated the solitary splendour of the spiritual leader of the Catholic world dressed in immaculate white. He blessed Urbi and Orbi. When he spoke, it was to speak of the

> … thick darkness has gathered over our squares, our streets and our cities; it has taken over our lives, filling everything with a deafening silence and a distressing void, that stops everything as it passes by; we feel it in the air, we notice in people's gestures, their glances give them away. We find ourselves afraid and lost. Like the disciples in the Gospel we were caught off guard by an unexpected, turbulent storm. We have realized that we are on the same boat, all of us fragile and disoriented, but at the same time important and needed, all of us called to row together, each of us in need of comforting the other. On this boat … are all of us.

His words spoke the brazen truth of what most of us had tried to suppress for weeks: a plague has descended upon humanity.

Eleven million televiewers watched this sombre television coverage to receive Pope Francis's blessing. I joined this faceless throng of global televiewers in the very late evening in Singapore while my body began to slowly feel the onset of the virus that already clung to my tissues. The fever had begun even while I dispelled the thought and passed it off as sunstroke from the late morning walk.

Now we know more than we ever did, that which we had always assumed as a taken-for-granted fact: social communion is at the core of our humanity.

Touch, feel and proximity is central to survival . . .

declared the psychoanalyst Susie Orbach. From the moment of birth, our socialization into a human community begins, and we learn the norms and rules by which we can live side by side without causing the destruction of the Other. In fact, due to this socialization, we learn how we might protect, preserve and propagate the Other. We form bonds, first with family, then with other beings outside our immediate, intimate circle. From an expanded community, we derive sustenance through communication. We learn the art of sharing, the circulatory process of giving and taking.

The eminent anthropologist, Marcel Mauss, who wrote *The Gift* in 1925, argued that exchange lies at the heart of all human societies, and reciprocation is the universal practice, whether of archaic tribes in Melanesia or corporate groups in the industrial northwest. A system of exchange and obligation keeps us linked to one another as we, in turn, maintain and reinforce these practices to ensure that our social ties are preserved. So we must, because upon the gift lies the perpetuation of the human species.

Under lockdown, this exchange was disrupted, this disjuncture in global human existence magnified. Pushed back into the cave, we resisted, screamed and kicked, wanting to come out. Longing to behold someone's face, caress a cheek, shake someone's hand, cling to an arm, perhaps even smell the whiff of newly shampooed hair from a passer-by. Share a meal, sign a contract. Horse-trade. Swap, snipe. Engage in mindless chatter.

In Italy, where one of the earliest rapid outbreaks occurred, there were simple cries for permission from city mayors to hold graduation parties, walk their dogs, provide services for taken-for-granted vanities through mobile hairdressers. Andrea Boccelli's solo performance inside an empty Milan Cathedral on Easter Sunday was gripping, both for the magnificent strength of his operatic voice that filled a vast emptiness, as well as our sharing the 'wounded Earth's pulsing heart.'

The cruelty of isolation is best appreciated in the extremes, like in the case of Albert Woodfox. He spent forty-three years in solitary confinement for the alleged murder of a prison guard in 1970. His sentence was considered the longest ever. It was finally overturned in 2016 after three rejected appeals. On 16 May 2016, he left West Feliciana Parish Detention Center in Louisiana the same day he turned sixty-nine years old.

Woodfox spoke of his determination to stay connected even under solitary confinement. He spent at least two hours a day outside his cell for forty-three years. He watched television documentaries and read newspapers during that time to stay in touch with the outside world. He battled creeping claustrophobia by sleeping upright with his mattress standing against the wall until the sweating stopped and the tomb-like feeling of being incarcerated in a 6 x 9-foot cell dissipated. He and his other two co-accused inmates, themselves found innocent and released, made a pact in 1972 that

> . . . we would never become institutionalized, . . . we made sure we always remained concerned about what was going on in society—that way we knew that we would never give up. I promised myself that I would not let them break me, not let them drive me insane.

This was the triumph of stubborn agency over cruel structure—the persistence of the oldest sociological tension—but in the extreme.

Whereas I endured isolation only for a day. On the sixth floor of Tan Tock Seng Hospital on the first day of confinement, I looked out from a vast expanse of the window that faced the driveway of the front entrance where other COVID suspects and I went through the screening process. When the results of my X-rays returned, I was wheeled into an isolation room. The tests followed immediately to rule out influenza and dengue. An antibiotic drip was inserted into the vein of my right hand to arrest the early signs of pneumonia. My doctors in plastic PPEs swished about, latex gloves worn, torn and discarded as they left the negative-pressure room. They conferred that I should remain in isolation until the swab results definitively established that I was infected with the virus.

Then all fell still and silent. The waiting game began.

When the results confirmed that I had contracted COVID, an hour of contact tracing on the phone from an official with the ministry of health promptly ensued. In my weakened feverish state, I recounted the guests at the Sunday barbecue, the taxicab driver at 2 a.m., the shuttle-bus driver who had tested positive a few days before, the supermarket visit from where I purchased a potted bluebell creeper plant, my husband already quarantined at home. Then I slept, for the first time in a decade, all alone.

In isolation, we are confronted with the nothingness of our existence. Schedules are upended. Conversations cease. Human contact evaporates. Alone, my interactive world shrank to a few characters of WhatsApp and Viber messages to my husband and my siblings scattered across the globe. Little remained that was of any import: not my research for a massive handbook project nor the regular socials with university colleagues; not the housekeeping routines nor the intellectual exchanges in seminar rooms. Connected through digital apps in a negative-pressure hospital room, my minimal human contact was reduced to short updates about COVID. Only COVID. Just COVID.

I moved down one floor after twenty-four hours in the hospital when it was established that my lungs were not impaired, and my symptoms were relatively mild. I had no cough nor cold, not even shortness of breath. Just fluctuating fever.

It was the same size room that I would inhabit with another patient. A shared bathroom posed initial squeamishness, but I had the bed closest to the window. My view was of the greenery on Jalan Tan Tock Seng Street rather than the nursing station on the opposite side of the room where my roommate's bed was located.

In that shared hospital space, I encountered my inner need for solitude. Living in close proximity to five strangers who were all discharged ahead of me forced me to locate my privacy.

Within a week of my hospital confinement, Singapore went into 'circuit-breaker mode', which meant an almost total curb on mobility. Infections in the migrant workers' dormitory were skyrocketing, and the government had to impose controls to immediately prevent an

overwhelming of the healthcare system. In addition, the hospital was
filling up with patients, detectable through the arrival of ambulances at
all hours of day and night. So, for however long I was going to remain
in the hospital, I would have to share the room with a constant intake
of patients.

This situation posted a delicious twist of irony: as COVID patients,
we were isolated in a negative-pressure room, totally detached from
the outside world. But two patients in very close proximity, separated
by a flimsy, yellow curtain, was my version of overcrowding. I heard
their snoring as they must have heard mine; the violent coughing of
more seriously afflicted patients made me cringe with the thought of
microbes released into our shared airspace; the tearful phone calls as
they spoke of their fears to their loved ones was always heart-rending;
the diagnosis of doctors who visited us both every morning unwittingly
letting us know the extent of the other person's illness; the nurses
who swabbed us and took our blood pressure and oximeter readings
at ungodly hours of day and night were an exercise in comparative
contagion.

I longed for silence and hoped that my roommate's mobile phone
batteries would die so that the marathon conversations, punctuated
by coughing and shrill laughter, would end. Awakened abruptly by my
roommate's loud snoring, I scrounged around for cotton balls to plug
my ears, to no avail. Even the slurping of soup and the munching
of afternoon biscuits sounded way too magnified, like there were
loudspeakers in my roommate's mouth as she ate the daily ration of
hospital meals.

The virus forced open our private worlds. I spoke to my mother
on Easter Sunday without video, so she would never know I was in
the hospital. My roommate then, the third one thus far, smiled at the
family subterfuge. She understood when I motioned with my forefinger
on my lips—a shared COVID secret. At the same time, her grandson
called her all hours of the day to plead with her to come home because
he needed his bedtime story. Over twenty-five days, I picked up on
family dynamics, culinary habits, fashion preferences, work disruptions
and dislocations—all without needing to eavesdrop.

Thus, I ventured to find solitude in the limited spaces of the hospital. On one occasion, when I awoke at daybreak, there was an unspeakably magnificent sunrise as I had not ever seen in Singapore in all the years I lived here. It started at 5 a.m. as a faint, red streak of colour stretched across the skyscrapers, then ever so gently rose into the sky, turning into a soft ecru colour. The glass windows of the buildings sparkled like tiny lemons. Finally, close to 8 a.m., the sun turned fiercely yellow as it beat down on the empty streets below, casting a sheen on grey pavement, lifting the desolation of abandoned concrete a tiny bit. There was no rush hour, and the sun rays were allowed to dance on the pavement undisturbed.

On other days, two birds would perch on the outside ledge of my window, their voices tiny, as if paying me a cheering-up visit to dispel my doubts and to reassure me that I would remain on this planet for a while longer. COVID would not snuff out my breath as of yet.

I inhaled these soundless gifts. Then, without form, I held those moments in my hands and stroked them into lingering. They reminded me of the prayer flags fluttering in the wind in a mountain shrine in Kathmandu. And the water from the Himalayas rushing down the stream in the middle of Thimphu in Bhutan. They were ephemeral energies that I stored in my hospital memories. One of my favourite writers, Pico Iyer, called them the 'eloquent sounds of silence'. During my hospital confinement, Pico Iyer's ruminations about silence and solitude spoke to me directly, and I was as enthralled and uplifted as the day I read it twenty years ago. Twenty-five days of near isolation in the hospital was a moment, albeit a short one, to appreciate that silence is, indeed, an eloquent voice.

Chapter 3

Breathing Again

My father passed away twenty years ago. He suffered for almost a decade from prolonged chronic obstructive pulmonary disease, what we in the family called emphysema. He was a heavy smoker in his younger days, a trademark of Filipino machismo. He clutched his unfiltered, Pall Mall cigarette like his precious personal toy, and he inhaled with gusto, especially after a rich meal with other equally heavy-smoking male friends. Standing tall with a cigarette held between two fingers, his posture was captured in a photograph in the 1960s when he was an accomplished engineer managing a large steel plant of over 2,000 employees. He must have felt every inch the epitome of a robust, virile, Filipino male. Until the pernicious effects of the disease caught up with him. A blessing, I thought, that he didn't live through COVID. He would not have survived the pandemic.

My father couldn't describe what he felt when his chest muscles were so constricted that his lungs felt squeezed. He gasped more than he could speak. His breath wheezed very loudly, at times sounding like a wounded stallion crying for relief.

His lungs were exhausted from the battering of incessant coughing. His chest muscles were shrunken, his shoulders hunched with his every effort to expel the accumulation of fluids. Progressively the illness overtook him even as he faithfully exercised discipline in ministering to his medicines and keeping watch over his diet. The oxygen tank and nebulizer were permanent fixtures in his bedroom. The Ventolin puff was always within reach. Two quick sprays and his breath would return, but never in full. Instead, he would inhale the air immediately surrounding him, like goldfish momentarily out of water.

As an aunt described it at a recent Sunday Zoom family gathering, perhaps 'breathing through a straw' summed it up rather accurately. As if she had just goaded me into an asthma attack, my breathing shortened all of a sudden. I switched off the video so that my mother would not see my heaving chest. I reached for my inhaler, took in two steroidal puffs and my thumping breath quietened. It took all of two decades and only after I got infected with COVID, that I understood, albeit inadequately, my father's long struggles with his breath.

For all of the ten years that my father suffered from chronic obstructive pulmonary disease (COPD), his children parachuted in and out of the Philippines, where he and my mother lived all of their lives. Frequent hospitalizations brought us together to urge him back to health. Then, one particular morning, my oldest brother called urgently to tell me to skip work and go to the hospital instead. I entered the hospital room; the mood was dark and heavy. I was sure of a shadowy presence behind the door. A silhouette with wings sharply pointed upward, like a mighty bird about to take flight, lingered and waited. Ominous but not frightening. I thought I saw the Angel of Death come to usher him away from this mortal world. And then I resisted and pleaded with the mysterious being. Not today. Not yet.

A few hours later, my younger brother brought his children from America. My father would love to see his grandchildren, perhaps find through them a motivation to last a while longer and watch them grow into the fullness of adulthood. In this, my brother's estimation was correct. He knew what fathers aspired for. At the end of a fairly long day that began with my father threatening to slip into a coma, we gathered close to him, three generations of us, into a small crowd around his hospital bed and lovingly coaxed him back to strength.

At dusk, the room brightened. The dark silhouette disappeared. My father returned to steady breathing. His voice was once again clear, strong and determined. He asked for a sponge bath from the male nurse who gave his scalp a good scrubbing. His cheeks flushed from the gentle heat of warm face towels. Patted dry and draped in a heavy cotton bathrobe, he was the image of total comfort as he began to scratch and peel the dry skin on his feet—a curious habit that was his trademark which we all inherited. We turned to one another and recognized the instinctive behaviour of someone who reverts to bodily habits when the dangerous moment passed. He picked and peeled his ankles and toes until a layer of softened skin appeared. Preserved and intact, he was back amongst us.

The grandchildren's voices rose in a babble of fast-trading jokes, many of them colloquial, corny and all-around incomprehensible. But we laughed nonetheless and rejoiced because my father held on to his life for eight hours and finally overcame the darkness. We then ordered his favourite dish—Vietnamese *pho* soup from across the street, hot and steaming, laden with tender beef strips, bean sprouts, flat rice-noodles and fresh basil. He ate and slurped. We joined in a hearty and thankful soup-slurping session to celebrate the extension of his life.

As far as memory serves me, this was his last severe episode when he managed to thwart the invitation from Death. As a result, there were no hospital confinements for about two years. Instead, he enjoyed a new stately home that my mother, a vigorous architect in her eighties, built for both of them. During the grand blessing, our closest friends marvelled at the stamina of my parents, who designed and constructed a magnificent dwelling in their advanced age.

My father spent mornings in the garden to drink in the warm sun and build up a healthy sweat. Then after a sponge bath that left him refreshed, he had his simple breakfast of boiled rice, fried eggs and occasional strips of beef or fish. On exceptional days when his breath was robust, he would raise his voice into a thundering crescendo, sometimes to scold the errant gardener; at other times to castigate the cook's inattention to his dietary needs; occasionally to berate me for being stingy with my time with him.

My yearning to finish graduate school returned, and I told him, once again, that I was leaving for Boston to finish my degree. My mindless detours through two failed marriages interrupted my intellectual quest. I promised him I had discarded all amorous adventures. The last leg of this PhD marathon would soon be completed. My restless identity search would come to a definitive conclusion as soon as I received the rolled parchment of paper with ornately printed calligraphy in Latin.

'Don't do this for me; do this for yourself,' his advice was poignant and unforgettable. 'I am happy with you, and I will always be proud of you. You don't need to prove yourself to me any more.'

So, I shut down my flat and reduced my belongings into two suitcases. I landed in Massachusetts on a showery, summer evening in late August, singularly focused on tackling graduate school again, determined to finish without further detours. My father was my weekend phone pal. I regaled him with stories of Boston—a place he will never come to see despite his wishes and my hopes that he hung on until I defended my thesis. Every summer and winter, I would go home for a visit, armed with his favourite 4711 cologne purchased from Brattle Street in Cambridge and packs of light biscuits for afternoon tea.

I had a few regrets, regrets that I've come to accept over the course of two decades, as the failures of a young adult who was much too preoccupied with her sense of self. I wish I had spent more time with him and lingered at the breakfast table for conversation instead of rushing off to work. I wish I had broken the unnecessary arguments and saw through them his need for tenderness instead. I wish I lived at my parents' home and gave up the quest for privacy, accomplishment and independence. I wish I were a better daughter. In remembrance, I still cringe at my shortcomings and try to find a place of forgiveness within.

In her pioneering book on the subject, Elaine Scarry wrote, pain is 'unshareable'. There is no language to reach our interior experiences. It is inexpressible, incommunicable. Pain destroys language, and sufferers are reduced to gasps, cries and moans in the most extreme instances.

Pain causes us to regress to a state anterior to language, to the sounds
and cries a human being makes before language is learned.

When my father died, I crumpled into a foetal position, unable to get
out of bed. It was cold, dank and dark in Boston when I returned
after the funeral. The February winter winds were forbidding, and my
resolve to finish my doctorate was evaporating. I wept alone. There
were no words, only an unfathomable void.

I called my sister on the West Coast often. We didn't talk very
much. Mostly we cried to each other on the phone—an intercontinental
sorrow that left us both diminished, bereft of all expressibility. But it
was the sorrow that bound us to each other. Unable to speak, sharing
telephone calls for months, hearing each other's sniffles, we found
some solace and the veil of sadness lifted very slowly.

Recalling those moments after I had contracted COVID, returned
the memories of my father's pain. Perhaps my glance into the possibility
of Death helped me find a language to share what I experienced, albeit
awkwardly.

However, I was nowhere near Death, I now believe, given my
mild episodic fevers and early pneumonia that was arrested within ten
days due to the returning strength of my immune system. So, even as
I entertained thoughts of dying during repeated positive results of a
stubborn virus that would not leave me, I was mainly convinced to go
back home, this time in a taxi, not in an ambulance.

After twenty-five days at the Tan Tock Seng hospital in Singapore,
I did return home. Leaving the controlled environment of the negative-
air-pressure room, the thick humid air immediately outside the hospital
room confronted me like the onset of a rushing wall of searing wet
heat. I felt I would choke. Within a few steps was the waiting room. I
collapsed into the nearest chair as I regained my breath and waited until
my suddenly dimming eyesight returned. My skin was turning clammily
cold, even as I was breaking out into a sweat. The sudden fatigue of a
few steps left me in disbelief. I fought against panic.

Weakened, thin, emaciated like a membrane, with sallow, sagging
skin on my forearms, ankles the size of children's bracelets, T-shirt

slipping off my shoulders, my feet one size smaller so my slip-on shoes flapped around them, I braved the few steps to the lift that brought me downstairs to the front of the hospital. Reaching the exit after a long, slow walk, I clung to the potted plant by the taxi stand, the exact same place where I had disembarked twenty-five days earlier when my corona journey began. Outside, I saw the vast expanse of blue sky, made fresh by the absence of vehicular traffic. Singapore was clean and spartan, still under 'circuit-breaker mode' that restricted mobility. We passed by a lone cyclist and a solitary jogger at the corner by my home.

It was twelve days after Easter. It did feel like a resurrection, and I was heading towards a new second life but within the same body, although very different as I would discover in the ensuing months. Like an old car with additional gears and wheels, I would have to befriend this body repeatedly with a whole new way of driving.

The bodily pains that ensued after my confinement would confuse me. Unwittingly, I stumbled upon the language of pain as I attempted to describe it to my general practitioner. Metaphor.

Starting at the right shoulder, the sensation felt like a rope creeping across my upper back, winding itself around muscle fibres and skin, tightening with every turn. The rope turned into a taut string as it reached for my nape, by which time I dared not turn my head. Then the string crept up my right cheek and pulled itself into a knot. I would hold my head straight, not wanting to move for fear of exacerbating the pain and encouraging the wire to constrict even more. I sat motionless, my jaws clenched, my eyes squeezed shut, as I slowly lifted two fingers to my temples to soften the creeping hardness across half of my face. I wondered what provoked this pain.

My breath would feel like it was entering and exiting a pipe at other times. All ten steps to the kitchen would leave me gasping. I could barely open the refrigerator door. Or, upon waking from a long afternoon nap, my right arm would feel limp and lifeless, as though the joint that connected it to my shoulder had come undone and my arm was a useless contraption. Finally, while sitting on the living-room sofa, a pain would stab the left side of my chest, and I would crumple.

On an evening when I felt an unusual surge of energy, I danced to Michael McDonald's 'What a Fool Believes', and as the song goes, 'trying hard to recreate what had yet to be created.' When the three-minute song ended, I grabbed the Ventolin inhaler for two micro-steroidal puffs. The dancing body I knew was of a distant past.

In a slight panic, when months passed without any let-up, I went to the emergency room knowing that I would be sent to the X-ray room for a closer look. Nothing turned up on the plates. No mangled tissues or torn ligaments. No dislocations. Everything was unremarkably normal, including the electrocardiogram that ruled out heart issues. I came home with pain killers and a tube of extra-potent anti-muscular-pain cream, still confounded by these inflammations that are traced to unknown causes. I am a long-haul COVID survivor.

A physician and professor of literature, David Biro, proposed metaphor as that connector between the subterranean experience of pain with the external world of experience. Himself having gone through a bone-marrow transplant, he described his pain that 'literally strangled his (my) vocal cords.' When we find the language to express our pain, the isolation ends and becomes 'as powerful as medicine, as soothing as a morphine drip.'

And so, we must strive to make visible that which is abstract, because pain is such an intrinsic and inescapable part of human existence. In finding language, we lift the dark shroud of incommunicability, end the isolation and remain immersed in a human community. Within the community, we converse; in conversation, we end the 'aching solitude' of pain, re-establish and strengthen even more our connection to humanity.

Returning to my father, now gone for two decades, I hope he hears me from the other side of reality. Not only because these physical pains that I endured on my road to recovery being the same as those he must have also suffered, but also because the pain we share from the different periods of our lives collapses time and distance and brings us close to each other again. He escaped the scourge of this virus. Were he alive today, he would have been utterly vulnerable, and the ruthless virus would have devoured him. The virus attacked me instead, and

I fought against it. Each day is an inch closer to recovery. However long this takes, I have risen above Death, battled my fears and confusion and continually find the language with which to appreciate the gift of my humanity even more. From where my father can hear me, he is undoubtedly beaming widely and cheering me on loudly. As when he visited me in my dreams a few days after he passed away, standing in the morning sun, meandering on Brattle Street in Cambridge, until he found the shop where I bought his favourite 4711 Cologne. His mortal body, now thoroughly shredded, he is breathing again.

Chapter 4

COVID Gardens

Ronald, my friend of over three decades, has turned into a 'plantito', the moniker given to born-again gardeners during the time of the pandemic. We swap photos of our greenery. However, my measly, pocket-sized gardens in my front and back balconies could never compete with Ronald's massive urban space in his ancestral home in the Philippines.

Eugenia, Jasmine and Magnolia would stir me to life in the mornings as Ronald sent over photos of his proud acquisitions. He made sure that each of them had a name so that, in caring for them, they became more alive and present, rather than mere stumps stuck in the soil.

The Madagascar palm, a *pachypodium lamerei*, is his latest addition. The cactus palm tree was the subject of a successful offensive towards an owner who wouldn't part with it. But he finally succumbed to Ronald's charm. As much as the Madagascar is a robust tree with a thick barrel stem covered with stout spines shooting up straight and determined, so was Ronald's unmitigated desire to purchase it. When Ronald decides, the mountains move.

I met Ronald in the heyday politics of the 1980s in the Philippines. We were all blown away by Corazon Aquino's victory through a peaceful, people-power uprising that ended the two-decade dictatorship of Ferdinand Marcos. Back then, both Ronald and I were younger political enthusiasts—he, a union organizer, ensuring that the social movements animated by the popular uprising would endure despite the demise of the dictatorship and the onset of a still-fragile democracy; me, an engaged sociologist, committed to teaching a future generation of students about the virtues of democracy. A shared background in student activism was a solid basis for our comradeship.

But it was only in December 1989, when Ronald was stranded in Amsterdam airport to catch the evening plane home to Manila, that our friendship was irrevocably sealed. An ongoing *coup d'etat* in Manila left him unable to board his plane. At Schiphol airport, he was frail and freezing, having survived a six-hour interrogation by Dutch immigration authorities who finally believed his story about the coup in Manila and the closed airport. He was given a one-week visa extension.

I was, at the time, going through a sordid and bitter divorce from my Dutch husband. The circumstances of our being in the Netherlands at the same time couldn't have been more incongruous, yet our friendship, by then almost a decade strong, was a warm blanket against the Dutch winter.

With all of ten Dutch guilders, the pre-Euro currency of the Netherlands at the time, we set off to find our familiar friends. A Filipino-French Trotskyite couple allowed us to live in their school, the International Institute for Research and Education—an 'ecosocialist' school, it called itself, dedicated to nurturing global activism.

'More like army barracks, very spartan,' quipped Ronald, as we were reminiscing over text messages during quarantine. He remembers how we were kept warm by the famous Dutch duvets and mulled red wine with cloves and cinnamon. In between ideological sparring over the varieties of socialism, some better than others, we slurped spaghetti, admonished by our hosts not to slice but to twirl the pasta around our forks. Hot conversations inside the school kept the bitter cold at bay.

We were a pair of Asian waifs looking every bit like unwitting refugees. Me, an emotional one, going through a nasty divorce; he, a temporary political exile, waiting for the Manila airport to reopen. We visited friends in The Hague, sipped tea and munched Dutch pastries with an Amsterdam-based, global think-tank director. We attended political fora on the ongoing coup in the Philippines. We listened to a Filipino exile who was a legend in the Left movement and whose ideas enamoured us during our student activist days.

'He looks more like a rich, Asian trader rather than a high-brow ideologue,' Ronald snickered. 'What a massive demystification.' His culinary adventurousness matched Ronald's irreverence. We sampled Dutch *bitterballen* and *poffertjes*—traditional Dutch croquettes and mini-pancakes—as we made our way back to the Trotskyite barracks while escalating Ronald's demolition of the Legend of the Left.

After that, he became my protector and bodyguard. My key informant. My confidant and adviser in matters of heart and mind. No one I harboured an interest in, whether strong or mild, would escape his scrutiny or his two-bits worth of worldly advice. At Starbucks, he once reproached me.

Ronald: Him? Why? He's tediously boring. None of your
          bohemian spirit.
Me: Huh? Nobody ever called me bohemian.
Ronald: That's why you get into trouble. Your wild spirit can't be
          tamed and shouldn't.
          He's strait-laced, staid. Junk him.

No topic was ever too insignificant, outlandish, or contentious to cause a breakdown in conversation. Our slight differences in social democracy and democratic socialism were, in the end, tedious hair-splitting.

He ventured to faraway Latin America to partake of the socialist experiments and brought back Brazilian coffee. I explored Asia, a vast enough region to satisfy my interest in Asian exotica. We swapped travel (mis)adventures and indulged in our common wanderlust.

We gossiped. We agreed on the peculiarities of common friends. Cared for the same persons who graced our paths even if some of them ended on opposite ends of the political spectrum. Despite his characteristic *machismo*, that affliction among Filipino males, Ronald was every bit a loyal, caring and affectionate human being. His bravado was a convenient prop, but his heart would quickly soften when confronted with human drama. Consistently, our friendship was like returning home, growing deeper and getting better with each new disclosed episode of our accumulating escapades.

When the pandemic struck, and I was hospitalized, Ronald was the first person outside of my family to whom I reported the unfortunate event. Every day for twenty-five days, he was my digital companion, my cheerleader, my informant about the world outside during the time that mine was reduced to a small hospital room. He related the brutality of Manila's lockdown—a gruelling seventy-five days when immobility was enforced by military checkpoints all over the city, resembling more like a war zone. He boasted about his valiant attempts to visit his mother to deliver her food and medicines. 'It's all a matter of stealth, wit and charm,' he said when confronted by the unwelcoming gestures of uniformed quarantine enforcers.

It must have been during one of those weeks of nonstop reporting on deaths among common friends that the exchange turned to gardening. Shocked by the untimely departure of those we knew well who had succumbed to COVID, we shifted our communication gears. We had had enough of such sordid news of friends and relatives who had yielded to the beckoning of death; some, the victims of the virus, others, of lingering ailments. All the same, it was an agonizing period for Ronald, whose time was spent attending vigils and funerals. And I, upon receiving the news in my hospital room, pondered my own mortality. We needed upliftment; we needed to be reminded of life. Determined and deliberate all at once to live and unwittingly pursue it more vigorously, we turned to gardening.

'Because planting is an act of life,' he mused. Then suddenly, it all came together, this passion in bloom.

He sent me the first photographs of two pots of *medinillas magnifica*, described by Wikipedia as 'showy rose grapes'. Indeed, these hanging, pastel-purple bulbs sat magnificently, like tiny empress dowagers poised atop marble stands, surrounded by yellow angels' trumpets and white Nicaraguan jasmine. Far into the corner were towering bamboos that give shade and shelter to marigolds and hibiscus. And where once there was a steel frame to serve as a security barrier to his home, now the cold encasement is a massive trellis for creepers, vines and air plants—all interlocked in an orgy of greenery.

A garden is that protected physical space, says Sue Martin-Smith, author of *The Well-Gardened Mind*, a place where time is of no relevance and one is cradled in the embrace of natural life. We return to them when we are overwhelmed by the onrush of living.

'They are refuges,' says the English writer and garden designer Mirabel Osler.

> We retreat to them as a safe haven . . . Gardens act as a solace and a panacea. With their innumerable qualities, we use them in a variety of ways, for inspiration or freedom, for discovery or surrender.

Or simply a chance to decompress from the long hours of computer work. Take a break from Word processing and watch instead an episode or two of *Gardener's World*. Monty Don, a British garden writer, has been hosting the show since 2003. A total of thirty-three episodes ran from March to October 2020. Since then, sales of seeds and gardening paraphernalia boomed in the UK and the United States. It's a kind of 'true counterprogramming', writes Steven Kurutz of the *New York Times*, who covered the story of Monty Don, the instant star all dressed up in overalls, woollen sweaters and muddy boots. Watching daffodils and bluebells on screen instead of labouring over Excel sheets became an 'oasis of normalcy, a balm for frayed nerves.'

A new season aired in March 2021, the pandemic's first anniversary. Produced by BBC, the show is now considered 'essential public service broadcasting', says executive producer Gary Broadhurst.

The social, natural and spiritual worlds meld into the garden as one continuous, seamless domain. Amid a green grove, we feel rooted almost literally, as when we are standing on a patch of soil and feel the earth with our bare feet.

In the garden, working with one's hands, stills the mind. There is a calmness to trimming a wayward branch of yellow palm to make room for new growth; or guiding a philodendron twirl itself and creep upwards along a stake. A solitary snail caught all of my attention for an entire hour, as it munched on spinach and bay leaves The love birds would return to build a nest at the highest point of our stone bamboo trees.

In the garden, my mind would never drift. Instead, it would focus singularly on the task of ensuring that the thin, thorny stem of the spreading bougainvillea would not break beneath the weight of my fingers. Then, as the last of the flowers were hoisted on a dry branch for support, my mind stopped the usual overdrive, forgetting for a while the anxieties of a prolonged COVID recovery.

My garden is a sanctuary that very few visit given its small size, enough only for two people to lounge for a tea break or an evening aperitif. Mostly, the early morning birds are its regular guests. I hear them from my bedroom window chirping to each other to welcome the morning when all around is empty of human movement. As they hop from leaf to branch, I realize that they are configuring the location of their prospective nest. The painstaking work of attaching twigs and shredded leaves with their saliva was a marvel to watch from a far distance inside my living room, not wanting to disturb this bit of urban delight. That they chose our balcony must have been because of the worms that crawl in and out of our potted plants—a regular source of food for the little one when the eggs hatch.

The relationship between plants and earth is like watching a mystery yield its secrets, so invisible that one has to gaze pointedly at the meeting of soil and seed, leaf and air, sun, shade and shadow. Each other's presence entices them. Yet their entanglements are soft and subtle, like whispers, droplets and drizzles.

One of my purple ruellias would not flower, went instead into a kind of lazy hibernation for about six months. Despite feeding her organic fertilizer and daily watering, she wouldn't bloom. I watched her often, waited for clues as to her desires. She seemed to have gone into a long nap and would not be hurried into waking up. Not unhappy, but not too cooperative either, I moved her across the balcony, all seven steps it took to re-position her at a spot where she could have the full morning sun, undisturbed in her corner space while she revelled in a daily sunbath. Since the transfer, she has produced anywhere between five to ten purple flowers each day. Her nap was finally over, and she was unstoppably blossoming!

Perhaps the joy of gardening lies in the intrinsic permission to co-create, a kind of 'procreative intercourse', as the American poet Stanley Kunitz called it. Planting is so unlike musical writing. Or painting. A blank sheet awaits the songwriter to inscribe the notes. The painter is faced with an empty canvas, ready for a deluge of design and colour that is all about executing the artist's conception. On the other hand, a garden is at once both empty and filled. The unseeded soil provides length, depth and breadth parameters—a patch of space that offers both constraint and possibility. Human hands mobilize a vision of growth to let the soil yield life; a mental design takes material shape.

In my rather narrow balcony, multiple bamboo branches bend as they hit the ceiling to form an indoor canopy, giving us a sense of graceful protection. Meanwhile, the bougainvillea grow past the ceiling and shoot outwards into the strong sunlight, shielding us from the human commotion outside our flat. A few medium-sized pots host *heliconias* while the smaller ones accommodate the flourishing rhododendron, mindful of the vertical space so she can spiral upwards.

But it is my brother-in-law's garden that epitomizes the power of co-creation. He and my sister, a self-confessed non-gardener, live in Silicon Valley, the birthplace of global digitalization. In the midst of dizzying innovation, he built a garden worthy of Eden. Over decades, he nursed a bay leaf tree, now a tall natural fence. They weave these leaves into aromatic wreaths for giveaways to their friends at Christmas time. Their bedroom looks out into a trellis of pink and yellow roses creeping upwards across the roof from the garden below. Their pocket-sized, front garden is adorned with perennials. In the spring, he experiments with narcissus bulbs. When entering their home, it is a small avalanche of colours and smells.

Their son, a scientist by day and an aspiring chef by night spends some of his Sundays at his parents' home, where he plucks fresh figs and lemons from the garden to produce homemade tarts as dessert after a family meal. On Zoom Sundays, my sister tours us into her garden so that we might imagine the freshness of lavender, tarragon, spring onions and basil. All of these end up, inevitably, on their dining table.

'Gardening is also about the forces of destruction,' says Sue Martin-Smith. First, there is the sudden, unexpected death due to mindlessness and simple inattention. As when the branches of my blue pea flowers dried up and died after months of harvesting blue pea flowers. These erotic blooms are freeze-dried and mixed into a tea concoction of calendula and rosebuds. One unsuspecting day, their stems turned pale brown and their leaves drooped. I had crowded them into a tiny pot, and they robbed each other of nutrients being planted so close to each other, as explained by one of my digital garden advisers. I should have re-potted them when their stems multiplied. Fortunately, the vines produce pods, and when dried, their pods open, and seeds fall into the soil, an uninterrupted cycle of growth and death. I've replanted the blue pea seeds. They have yielded flowers again, albeit slowly, to emphasize that this would be my newfound lesson at attentiveness and patience. The flowers are in no rush. They will bloom again in due course, I suspect, when I have learned to treat them more delicately.

In today's hyper-mobile existence, gardens are places for slowing down and standing still. During times when my life was a series of relocating countries, changing addresses and transferring homes, I sought to create a garden in all of them. My search for a flat was always with an outdoor area for sitting, lounging, napping and planting.

A particular flat in Bangkok where I lived in 2007 for a whole year had a wrap-around balcony in the middle of the city's central business district. Wanting to waste no time, I ventured to Chatuchak district, Bangkok's famous outdoor market. I outfitted the balconies with trees and flowerpots to mute the noise from vehicular traffic and shielded my view from the hotel and office complex directly across my bedroom. Wide-mouthed open terracotta pots, hosting numerous water lilies and lotuses, burst into colours of purple, white and fuchsia as they drank in the punishing heat of Bangkok's sun. These water flowers were complimented by towering African Nile papyruses, standing alongside a row of bamboo hedge plants. In the shaded areas by the kitchen were rows of white anthuriums and cala lilies whose blooms muted the stark grey walls of a tailoring shop, a mini mall and the imposing tower of the Conrad Hotel. I splurged on tropical orchids to grace my living room, brought every late afternoon by a vendor with a flower pushcart.

But it was the healing power of gardening that was the true hallmark of my Bangkok sojourn. I discovered the power of gardening for emotional restoration and upliftment by nursing a wounded heart from a nasty breakup, coupled with a fear that my professional worth had collapsed. I fled to Bangkok to rebuild my heart, head and home.

On a cool January morning in 2007, when I opened the sliding doors of the balcony in my newly occupied flat, two white butterflies flew straight at me and lightly kissed my left shoulder. Then, in a fraction of a second, they both flew back into the morning air, two tiny phantom angels welcoming me into a life that was to begin anew. Awesome and ominous. I had come to the right place.

I purchased several pots of birds-of-paradise known for their thick, hardy stems and spectacular colours of flowers that resemble cranes in flight. They grow in clumps with leaves like those of the banana tree, heavy and sturdy to hold the flowers upright. They flourish without much prodding and bloom on the sly. There would be a whole array of them one day, displaying their magnificence in striking blue and orange colours. Maybe I tended them as a subconscious reminder of my need to quickly re-establish my emotional strength, poise, stability and equanimity and re-emerge a sturdier being from this painful episode. I did. When I closed down the apartment in 2008 and relocated to Singapore a year after I ended my emotional exile, I had reinstated my faith in my ability to compete professionally once again successfully, and I re-entered the world of academe in one of Asia's top universities. I gave the plants to friends in Bangkok as a gift of restoration, arriving in Singapore with the history of pain and loss firmly behind me. The Bangkok garden taught me about emotions going underground but without suppression, tending and taming them into quietude until they are smoothed over and soothed by the creative power of gardening. The painful past was firmly buried.

During the pandemic, we turned to gardening to befriend the silence and isolation of quarantine. And perhaps to be transformed by it as well. I recognize it in Ronald, my activist friend with a passion for collecting guns, swords, antique knives. That was pre-pandemic behaviour. 'I have stopped going to the firing range for practice shooting,' he said. Instead, he drives around his neighbourhood in search of green bargains. He's hoping to chance upon a rubber tree, those robust un-fussy species that clean up the environment while standing in place, like a silent sentinel going about its own business without fanfare.

'I have four pots of them,' I said to him. 'Too bad I can't ship them to Manila. I would happily give you one.'

So, he displays his Madagascar trees instead. He has grown very fond of them and has even struck a friendship with the avid collector/owner.

'By accident, I found him,' he said, 'while driving around and spotting them from my car.' He convinced the owner to part with three more trees, smaller ones that will need care and tending to. He accidentally pricked his finger on one of its thorny spines on one occasion.

'It was a week of pain before it disappeared,' he said. 'Venomous. That's why they're my favourite. Awesome, dangerous. Just looking at them, I can already sense the danger and excitement. That's their fatal attraction.'

'Like you,' I confirmed, 'upright, bold, committed, dangerous when crossed, but never coarse, always elegant. You are never one or the other. That's your charm too.'

The texting exchange fell silent of a sudden. I had embarrassed him, I am sure.

At heart, Ronald is shy despite his bravado. Very much like the *mimosa pudica*, commonly known as the shrinking plant. Its leaves fold into each other when touched. *Makahiya* in our language. As children, we loved to tease their leaves into folding inward, like a kind of prayerful bashfulness.

Every day, as Ronald digitally reaches out to close the physical distance between us, now enforced by months of lockdown, quarantine and travel bans, he assumes his gardening posture, reviews his green empire and muses over additions to an expanding grove. We regale each other with talk of roots, tendrils and ferns interspersed with philosophical musings about life and death, growth and decay, aggression and tenderness. All the while connecting these abstractions with the firm material reality of our gardens in continuous growth.

When COVID cases hit 15,000 in one day, Ronald sent the latest update of his blooming flowers, both from his latest addition of succulents. 'There is still some beauty to behold in all this fear. I am not that brave; I am only pretending to be so. But beauty never fails to help me manage my fear,' he texted.

Breathlessly soothing surroundings and a much more tender being than I have ever known him for over three decades, Ronald is fully attentive and caring, born out of procreative intercourse between him and Nature.

He has always been astutely ecological, I am convinced. All it needed was a virus to prod him into activating his gardening DNA and begin his dance with Nature.

Two years later, as the pandemic receded, my green enthusiasm continues. My tiny, front balcony has an overhead trellis and the philodendrons twirl around the thick branches. Prints of the Russian painter Vladimir Tretchikoff grace the narrow walls of the entrance to our flat. A wooden figurine of a goddess sits in a graceful pose as she guards our home. Three tall bamboo branches have crept outside of the wrought iron railings to receive their daily dose of direct morning sunlight. A rattan armchair allows me precious moments to sit and marvel at this miniature forest I have built, as a testament to our human determination to rebuild life in the midst of disease and death. And like the *makahiya*, to fold my hands in a thankful prayer.

Chapter 5

From Analog to Digital: The Body and the Pandemic

Three and a half weeks of hospital diet was the best weight-control programme for me. Consuming about 500 calories a day, I achieved, without effort, near-perfect (to me) body weight. My skinny arms and legs, the size of chicken feet, flailed around the hospital bed as I pulled up the sheets to keep out the chill from the air-conditioning. My shrunken face disappeared into a mountain of pillows. My wrist yielded to the encirclement of my thumb and third finger, the front of my neck cradled snugly in the palm of my hand. There was no flab anywhere, just tendons, sinews and little bits of muscle, all held together by sallow skin.

Much to my delight, my hospital-issued cotton pyjamas hung about me in remembrance of Twiggy, the British cultural icon of the 1960s who weighed all of 91 lbs. In our late teens, we all aspired and conspired to achieve her gamine features, doe eyes, pouting lips, bony shoulders, long, thick (false) eyelashes, loose-fitting boyish clothes—an aesthetic of scrawny androgyny. There was nothing sartorially elegant about hospital gear; however, I was content with daily consumption of hospital fare if that reduced my physique and squared with my body image of extreme thinness. Like Twiggy, fifty years later.

Actually, I was dangerously emaciated. My immune system had just taken a beating. COVID had assaulted my lungs and weakened them. My lips were bluish, and my enlarged eyeballs seemed to pop out of their sockets. I lost massive amounts of hair, I'm convinced, from hydroxychloroquine. And my appetite hibernated for nearly a month. Rather than Twiggy, I looked more like a poster girl for a fund-raising campaign for famine.

My doctor roused me into a sudden panic with his announcement that my roommate had suspected tuberculosis. He called for my transfer into another room while we waited for my second negative COVID test. Walking in with coronavirus and walking out with mycobacterium was an abhorrent idea. I didn't fight this hard only to get afflicted by another deadly microbe. That would be life's cruel joke.

Upon his pronouncement, I sprang into a disavowal of vanity. My war on weight was over. I returned home with a firm rejection of the 1960s countercultural revolution on the body. So did Twiggy, by the way, when she famously said,

. . . you can't be a clothes hanger for your entire life . . .

after four years of modelling. She was twenty-one years old by then and finished with the body image, anxieties and obsessions among women. A final quip: 'Back in the 60s, there was a car sticker that read: "Forget Oxfam, feed Twiggy." But I ate like a horse.' Emulating her, I ate like a horse myself. My first meal upon arriving home: four-cheese pizzas, fried chicken wings and ice cream.

Long before corona, the battle against our bodies already raged. Our forebears taught us various traditions. The promotion and preservation of beauty are one of them. Physical attributes were our tickets to success variously defined: landing the ideal marriage partner, clinching the job interview, modelling as a career choice, acquiring celebrity status. Our body was a walking calling card, a condensed version of our biodata. We wouldn't merit a second glance from anyone if we failed the standards of beauty defined by the 1960s cultural moment that designated these standards: tall, skinny, white and bosomy.

'Will this be the last generation to have bodies that are familiar to us?' was Susie Orbach's provocative title in a late 2019 op-ed in the *Guardian*. Where once our bodies were biological organisms with limits that we by and large accepted, today, these limits are challenged,

> . . . stretched and pressed into new forms of service, display and identity . . .

thanks to omnipresent social media and an expansive empire of cosmetology.

My grandfather, a stalwart of the late 1900s who passed away during the turbulent period of women's liberation in the 1960s, admonished me regularly about the virtues of beauty and bashfulness. These were my assets in the marriage market, he insisted. He went about dispensing a regular lecture to his female grandchildren, all twenty of us, to remind us that nail polish, hairspray, lipstick and mini-skirts were the banes of the modern era. My grandfather castigated his daughter, my mother, then an accomplished professional architect in her own right, for wearing capri pants whenever she went to the job site to supervise the construction of residential homes and office buildings for which she became famous. During his pre-60s cultural moment, beautiful women never wore pants.

My grandfather clung to the image of Maria Clara—the apotheosis of feminine beauty—refined, shy, virginal. Like my grandmother, whom he married when she was eighteen. At the time of their courtship, they would meet in her home with a Spanish veil across her face, as the chaperones stood by to ensure propriety. Their conversations were whispers, which aroused in him a desire to reach out to her and plant an unwanted kiss on her cheek. Soon after, they got married. His impulsiveness had no place in a historical context when men were required to demand, preserve and protect a woman's unsullied honour.

He harboured illusions of my being married off to a high-society businessman or politician. So, his version of education for girls was more like finishing school. Proper female etiquette, household management, crochet and piano lessons so I could softly step on the pedal and run my nimble fingers across the ivory keys while regaling my husband with soothing melodies when he came home at night.

Educated in the Spanish tradition of the arts and letters in the late 1900s, my grandfather acquired the cultural mindset of Latin machismo, believing in the male's right to appropriate the female body, to shape and bend according to his will. Caught up in the transition to Americanism by the time his children were born, he cursed and ranted against a liberal education that allowed women into the classroom, let alone permitted them to pursue university degrees of their choice. My mother and aunt were the most highly educated in his family of two daughters and five sons. They were adamant about acquiring an education. Both pursued university degrees under two foreign occupiers—the Japanese and the Americans—who bombed their universities. Determined to finish their studies, both women returned to the university and graduated shortly after World War II.

In my generation, the body slowly moved into the realm of my control, not without struggle. Three brothers would occasionally frown on the presentation of my bodily self. Long hair, bell-bottomed jeans, close-fitting T-shirts, mini-skirts, hot pants—this was the 1970s decade of flower power and activism. Non-conformity, rebellion against established authority and women's lib were the order of the day. I repeated the American women's slogan 'burn the bra!' with my equally enamoured female classmates on the quick-rising global feminist agenda. We smoked Virginia Slims, the cigarette-of-choice for the new smokers' market—women. We were exposed to sex education and contraceptive pills, the latter a clever medical invention that bypassed my mother to her dismay. She lamented how she could have spaced her pregnancies and controlled the pace of her professional growth.

Joining the activists in the 1970s, the assertion of control over my body became more pronounced. I was growing up with an inner ferment, and I liked challenging the world into which I was born. The world was malleable, and I could change it. What enthralled me about activism, apart from the commitment to causes larger than oneself, is the personal efficacy I had come to obtain, a negation of the 'givenness' of life, which, up until then, was the cultural norm I had lived by.

So, I shed my pristine, green-and-white, school uniform and opted for faded jeans, T-shirts and worn-out sneakers. I alighted from the family car that took me to school daily, at a far enough distance from our activist headquarters, and walked the rest of the way so that I would not be seen in my bourgeois trappings. To be convincing about my commitment to the poor, I had to 'wear' the part.

My grandfather, a stern septuagenarian by then, suffered from utter dissonance. He couldn't quite get it. The modern women that he railed against were coiffed and painted. At the same time, I wanted to emulate the proletariat. To be modern included turning away from class privilege, rejecting the bourgeois standards of beauty and crafting an identity of my choosing, including how I wanted my body to look and what I wanted to drape it with. He and I could not reconcile these conflicting meanings of being a woman. He didn't have time and I didn't have the patience. He lived and died during a cultural moment of struggle when women rebelled against men like him.

At the close of the old century, the body became malleable, susceptible to manipulation. The battle waged on the body acquired new dimensions as technology and medical advances opened up dizzying possibilities: embryo implantation; parental surrogacy; liposuction; cryofreeze; radiofrequency lipolysis; eyelid blepharoplasty; breast enlargement; genital reconstruction; organ transplants; stem-cell harvesting and storage; umbilical-cord preservation.

'*Wala nang pangit ngayon* (there are no more ugly people today),' my mother jokingly declared the end of physical imperfection, however minor or major. Every unwanted fold and freckle can be fixed, every deformity corrected. There is no need to rush into old age. So, she admonished her daughters, what with techniques for restoring collagen, facial peels, laser-guided wrinkle erasers.

'My favourite telenovela actresses are ageless,' she says admiringly. Every season they seem to become more and more gorgeous. Never mind if they can't act; never mind if the delivery of actors' lines is thin and contrived; never mind if the storyline is a poorly executed attempt at creative drama. Theatrical talent is secondary. But the visceral images of astoundingly beautiful faces are testimonials to the skilled and sensitive handiwork of cosmetic surgeons who work like furniture-makers behind the scenes to craft the perfect look.

Over drinks at an outdoor bar some years back, two male colleagues were very discreetly communicating hand signals to each other on what they thought were 'body jobs' of the woman sitting next to our table. Then, they started on her lip-volumizing procedure, given her unnatural-looking pout.

'Like she was perpetually sulking,' one of them remarked.

And overstretched skin around the corner of her eyes, 'shiny and waxed like a doll,' said the other.

It was a game they played for hours. Her eyebrows and hairline, her neck, jowl and bosom did not escape their scrutiny. They surveyed her like a ship captain and his cartographer out in the ocean, anticipating the sight of dry land.

I reproached them in the taxi on our way home. 'So, do you talk about me like that as well?'

'Nah,' they replied through heavy beer breaths. 'Your wrinkles are visible.' My eyes widened, my brows raised in alarm, over this assault on my vanity.

'But charming,' said the other, quick to recover.

'You wear your wrinkles well,' was their parting shot before they dropped me off.

The marketplace for physical enhancement has exploded, undergirded by an ideology that hails the conquest of Nature. The body in late capitalism is a conquerable terrain. With all the available tools for body redesign according to some culturally derived template of desirability, the body can be entirely remade.

Women who have bought into this ideology spend hours surfing the cosmetic marketplace. Malls and department stores have multiple counters for enhancement products and processes. There are make-up sample sessions that include eyebrow-microblading, lip-contouring, cheek-shadowing, eyelash-lengthening, jawbone redefining. 'One can look stunning,' says an ad, 'why not look sensational instead?'

The technology boom projected our physical bodies onscreen. Too real, too present, too overblown. Every facial twitch and furrowed brow, the slightest creeping wrinkle, the hanging jowl and the sagging neck; the morning eye bags, the receding forehead, the unbrushed hair—all of life's bodily imperfections, digitally registered. In an instant, our appearances are on full display—the slant of our eyes, the hue of our skin, the angle of our cheekbones, the volume of our lips. It's a short guessing game of our cultural 'givens'—our ethnicity, geography and social status/social class are all articulated in a single facial image. The battle for manufactured perfection begins.

Thanks to technology, we can redesign ourselves into images of our choice: an avatar; an Emoji; a photograph of physical perfection—photoshopped, dramatized, stylized, reinterpreted, recreated, cartoonized, caricatured. The material body has been destabilized, the terms of engagement with our body permanently transformed with apps on our smartphones. Who knows today what we are really like?

Fast forward to early 2020. The pandemic shut down the temples of corporeal worship. Considered as super-spreaders, beauty salons, spas and gyms closed. No one was allowed a massage, a facial, a perm, or a haircut. Bodybuilding became a private affair. Public displays of pecs and abs stopped. Strutting around and showing off the excesses of body-sculpting went off-stage.

The ban on the body yielded horrendous, if not tragically humorous, proportions. Mayor Antonio Tutolo of Lucera disallowed mobile hairdressers in early 2020 as viral infection swept across Italy.

'What the hell is that?' he barked into the camera. 'Do you even know that the casket will be closed? Who the hell is even supposed to see you with your hair all done in the casket?'

Choir singing, considered a super spreader, was disallowed. A *Huffington Post* piece in July 2020 provided details of choir practice in Skagit, Washington state. Out of sixty-one avid singers, thirty-one were confirmed positive with COVID-19; twenty-one had 'probable' causes; three were hospitalized and two died. In Amsterdam, 102 of 130 choir singers fell ill after a performance. Three ended up in intensive care and one died.

According to the European Centre for Disease Prevention and Control, the virus could travel further during power singing. Loud speech and singing produce more respiratory droplets. These droplets could travel like projectiles, the virus hanging on to them until they land in someone's respiratory tract.

Power vocals are assets only if you are a solo star during a pandemic. Like Andrea Bocelli, whose performance in an empty Milan Cathedral at Easter, wrote Chris Willman of *Variety,* was hailed as the

> . . . signature cultural event of the pandemic, transcend(ing) religion, nationality, age demographic and even musical preference.

Concerts were cancelled and migrated to YouTube. Musical enjoyment retreated behind closed doors.

COVID transformed us into pixelated presences overnight. We are facial displays on a monitor with background enhancements of our choice. The virus hastened our entrance into the world of image processing, printing, manipulation, compression, representation, storage. Our bodies, the only bodily vessel we've inhabited before COVID, are now a 22-inch-monitor presence, spaced equidistantly by Zoom.

We've had online happy hour with friends in England; Zoom coffee and tea breaks with friends across the island; lunch with my mother in Manila; breakfast with my sister in Brussels; nightcaps with siblings in New York and California. We have regular Sunday family meals across the digital globe. At the head of the table, my mother sits by herself. We are all munching in front of our monitors. We've been 'dematerialized'; we've become digital habitués.

Then there's body surveillance. The demand for swift and early tracking has spurred technological advances in contact tracing. For example, in the earliest days of the viral spread in Singapore, each exposed person received a telephone call thrice a day for temperature checks while under a mandatory fourteen-day quarantine. In addition, contact tracers conducted hour-long interviews to establish a pattern of mobility and contact.

Two telephone calls in the afternoon of my first day of hospital confinement was an exercise in memory-digging. I had to establish the routes of the taxis and the shuttle bus, pick-up and drop-off points; the bus passengers, the hours of travel, the names of the transport companies. Then the interrogation of guests on a Sunday afternoon barbecue which I attended. All of them had to be located; their contacts thereafter had to be chased after as well. A network of potentially infectious persons had to be identified before the network expanded outward. In early April 2020, contact tracing became a kind of pre-Easter egg-hunt.

Within three months, the TraceTogether app was launched. Bar codes in smartphones took over phone calls. Finger swiping on one's mobile phone is the most practised gesture today to check our daily contacts. A logbook provides the number of Bluetooth exchanges with other TraceTogether devices within ten-metre distances for fourteen days. It's a Bluetooth 'handshake' says the TraceTogether website, capable of connecting to multiple Bluetooth devices and can travel through walls, ceilings, floors. Even while sitting at home in my improvised office, my electronic tracer picks up the gardener sweeping the debris outside my window, the family members en route to the swimming pool, the tenant in the next building passing through our common corridor. I would receive a text message if any one of them were infected. Meanwhile, I haven't moved one inch from my office chair.

Light consumer wearables such as the Apple Watch now have heart rate and physical activity monitoring. Pulse oximeters to measure blood oxygen have become household devices alongside the ubiquitous thermometer. A body sensor attached to one's upper arm can record fluctuations in blood glucose. It's safe to use in the swimming pool. A similar sensor the size of a Band-aid plaster can be attached at the base of the neck to capture recordings of wheezing and sneezing, heart rate, heart sounds and skin temperature.

The body in a pandemic is the subject of intense monitoring, technology its handmaiden. Continuous body-sensing was the subject of an editorial in the journal *Science Advances*. Three scientists, Hyoyoung

Jeong, John A. Rogers and Shuai Xu, advocated for the development
and use of consumer wearables. They are called 'on-body skin-
integrated sensor systems that couple intimately to the skin at locations
beyond the wrist and the finger.' These wearables are the emerging
fashion statements of the near future and are awaiting clearance for
release into the US market.

The virus has fast-forwarded human life that, as Susie Orbach
observes, will be 'constituted by algorithms and synthetic biology'—
processes that will increasingly render the physical body as outmoded,
dilapidated, unreliable. Perhaps. As we continuously adapt to
increasingly different visions of the future in which technology features
predominantly, the question that we ponder today as a human species
is when, if at all, can we physically meet and touch each other again.

As for my own body, COVID beat it up quite badly that I haven't
had a thought for reconstructing it. After a full year of social hibernation,
I was ready to brave an adventure to the hairdresser. A nice quick
trim to tame my unruly and overgrown locks was the summary of my
vanity. My lungs were intact, and I could inhale and exhale again. That
alone was sufficient.

Chapter 6

The Good Samaritans

On 25 April 2020, the Channel News Asia ran a story about a twenty-year-old student-entrepreneur, Ray, whose successful two-month-old *beehoon* (noodle) business was forced to shut down due to the circuit breaker in Singapore. He had poured all his savings into the venture, along with three school friends whose combined contribution was 5 per cent of the total investment. On 24 February 2020, Ray and his friends launched RaydyBeehoon. The stall was set up at the grounds of the Nanyang Technological University in Singapore and was located at Canteen 13.

Then COVID-19 hit Singapore. The stall had to close down when students living on campus moved out. Ray's customer base collapsed, and he was left with an empty stall and a nipped-in-the-bud business venture.

Undeterred, Ray and his friends shifted gears. They had plenty of energy and free time. They decided to continue cooking and distribute the noodle packets to the needy, especially the elderly. They went into fund-raising to cover the costs of ingredients, packaging and delivery. They expanded their cooking and distribution centres to all parts of the island and hooked up with a charity organization, Food Bank, to help distribute the noodles. A final touch was added to the noodle packets: three-ply masks which the elderly could most likely not afford given the cost, and therefore resorted to single-ply masks which were not very effective to protect against the virus.

His operation enticed an army of volunteers who drove their own cars (their parents' mostly) to distribute the food. He inherited two chefs whose businesses had also closed down during the circuit breaker.

From a modest $40,000 (approx. US$30,000) goal, the group raised $163,000 (approx. US$120,000) from over 1,400 donors at the end of the circuit break in mid-June. On Instagram, he announced that he was no longer accepting donations and is looking for other charities to donate the excess funds raised.

'Our hearts are full,' says Ray Sheng at the end of the article. And so was mine when I read this in my hospital bed, waiting to completely shed the viral load.

As were so many others. His Facebook page was inundated with questions on how they could help. He had more offers to volunteer than he had space for. His stall could only accommodate four people.

These were very young men and women who looked at the lockdown as an opportunity to, in their words, 'give back to society'. They were full-time students who juggled studying on Zoom with cooking, buying supplies, packing noodles, distributing these to the Food Bank.

I lay on my hospital bed in wonder: what did these kids just do? And why?

As altruist, Kristen Renwick Monroe, argues in her book, *The Heart of Altruism*, and has a different perspective from most others who live and believe in self-interest. Derived from the Latin word 'alter' meaning 'other', altruists harbour an overarching view of humanity—all of humanity—regardless of any and all social, cultural, physical attributes. The sociologist, Auguste Comte, coined the term to signify human conduct that primarily regards the good of others as the end of moral action. Where one sees a stranger, an altruist sees a fellow human being. It's the simplest of all equations as laid out in the Gospel of St Luke in the Christian Bible. Not a Jew, not a Levite, but a person in need was what the Samaritan saw lying on the roadside.

William D. Hamilton believed otherwise. If there was any altruism to be had in this world, it was due to kin selection—a strategy of helping out others in order to enhance the reproduction of one's relatives through 'help-inducing genes'. The spread of these genes produces an important kind of reproductive compensation so that the genes indirectly propagate copies of itself in those relatives even if there is a cost to the reproduction (e.g., the gene-spreader dies). These genes, when directed towards non-descendant relatives, like siblings and cousins, produce a sufficiently strong though indirect positive effect. Altruism spreads throughout the gene pool to propagate copies of itself. Clavien and Chapuisat terms it 'nepotistic altruism'. Simply put, it's self-cloning premised on the (perhaps mistaken) belief that you are a worthwhile human being whose existence should be continued.

Fair enough. Why shouldn't vanity be at the root of kin altruism if it leads to its own perpetuation? Why shouldn't my parents and siblings want me to be as good-looking as our first- and second-degree cousins?

I understood, somewhat, after these many years, why clan reunions were oftentimes long, showy affairs. Each yearly gathering was an opportunity to showcase the improvements—physical and otherwise—among clan members, whether these be choices of partners with desirable genes or improvements in one's physique despite the passage of years. And an occasion to made snide remarks about how someone else's genetic traits didn't quite improve our gene pool, when deterioration starts showing up in physical quirks and tics, or when a generation of children didn't turn out too sharp and savvy. What happened to the brainy cousin who's now limping across the floor? Or the once-elegant uncle who now humorously seems to be losing his marbles?

Further, I understood why my mother engaged in perpetual matchmaking with the sons of her upper-social-crust friends she deemed were fitting spouses to us, her daughters. They were good-looking, hence, favourably genetically reproducible; plus, they had the appropriate cultural standing. The convergence of genetic and socio-cultural traits ensured her a kind of perpetuity. After she departs this mortal world, her traits will endure and be propagated in succeeding generations. She, Hamilton would argue, was engaging in kin altruism. That I resisted her match-making efforts was not out of any disagreement with Hamilton whom I hadn't encountered at the time, but rather, on my entrenched liberal framework that I should have complete control over my genes and how they should be dispersed. In the end, I chose to keep my genes to myself, preferring not to reproduce myself. So there goes Hamilton who, I guess, did not quite anticipate that certain kin members may prefer not to contribute to gene photocopying.

To make further sense of my family's quirky traits, I resorted to the so-called calculus of utility which underpinned much of social theory. (Side note: lockdown is great for esoteric reading.) Rational-choice theory explains, nay, predicts human behaviour through the prism of functional utility and the promotion of self-interest. Economists have had a field day of it. Charts of demand and supply curves simplify human choices. Equilibrium price—the point at which supply-and-demand curves intersect—clear the market. The consumer made a rational choice. This axiom lies at the centre of homo oeconomicus—the economic (wo)man—a figurative universal human being who, as John Stuart Mill claimed in 1836,

> . . . desires to possess wealth, and who is capable of judging the comparative efficacy of means for obtaining that end.

The self-interested human permeates and predominates most of the social sciences particularly economics, political economy, political science, evolutionary biology and psychology.

But even the most ardent followers of rational calculation admitted to its flaws. Adam Smith, considered the architect of the theory of competitive capitalism, yielded to the notion of 'sympathy'. In his famous work *The Theory of Moral Sentiments* written in 1759, Smith asserted that,

> How selfish soever man may be supposed, there are evidently some principles in his nature, which interest him in the fortunes of others, and

render their happiness necessary to him, though he derives nothing from it, except the pleasure of seeing it. Of this kind is pity or compassion, the emotion which we feel for the misery of others, when we either see it, or are made to conceive it in a very lively manner . . . The greatest ruffian, the most hardened violator of the laws of society, is not altogether without it.

A century later, the German ethnographer, ethnologist and medical doctor, Adolf Bastian, proposed the idea of the 'psychic unity of mankind' in 1860. A well-travelled and highly eccentric professor of ethnology at the University of Berlin, Bastian emphasized that all cultures, regardless of variations in myths, beliefs and customs, share *Elementargedanken* (basic ideas) that are universal, transcultural and transhistorical. Later, the psychoanalyst, Carl Jung's idea of the collective unconscious was largely derived from Bastian's notion of mankind's basic unity. Jung's proposal of universal themes and images which he termed 'archetypes' enjoyed common threads with the claims of Adam Smith and Adolf Bastian that humankind shares universal mental and psychological bonds despite differing cultural manifestations. In these various works, one detects the stirrings of the idea of altruism, grounded in a belief of the universal bond of humanity. Auguste Comte joined in the chorus. In 1852, the word altruism entered the human lexicon.

Returning to Kristen Renwick Monroe: Altruists are different in their perceptual cognition especially the individual's perceptions of themselves in relation to others. These differences are explained by a host of factors like individual life-experiences and identity choices formed around group experiences. We might all have been schooled in Freudian psychology that posits self-gratification as the primary human motivation, or in Hobbesian political theory that emphasizes the world as a nasty, brutish place. However, our experiences with other people and other groups might suggest otherwise, and these experiences reshape our ideas. In turn, our cognition of the world changes; our perceptions of ourselves and of the Other change as well. Altogether, these perceptions guide our behaviour.

What a relief. We are not, after all, hostage to the baser instincts of pure self-promotion. We can and do help ourselves to become better than our original programming, genetic and otherwise. The Russian-American sociologist, Pitirim Sorokin, considered one of the founders of American sociology, argued that, despite our rationality, there are 'levers' to balance and curb the excesses of calculating tendencies. He called it solidarity. Humans are wired for compassion and sympathy towards other humans because of solidarity.

Humanitarian aid workers during the Ebola outbreak in Africa in 2014 exemplify this cognition and sense of solidarity. Alongside commitment, purposefulness and a strong moral identity, humanitarians decide to engage in endeavours even if these prove to be high-risk to the self. Lynne McCormack's study of humanitarian aid workers in Sierra Leonne during the Ebola virus outbreak confirmed that the overriding theme among humanitarians was one of benevolence and an existential belief in the oneness of humanity.

'I have a big thing about people not dying alone,' said one humanitarian.

Chimed another: 'I cannot save you, but I am here.'

And then another: 'If I do not go, who will?'

What the coronavirus achieved, apart from the continuing misery of threatening us all with prolonged illness, is the surfacing of these parts of us that might have lain dormant over years of quick-and-easy gratification. Under lockdown, resisting the urge to go stir crazy, or moved by the scale of seriousness wrought by the virus, many in quarantine formed online groups to support feeding programmes in places in the world where the virus caused many communities to suffer from lack of food supply.

Electronic groups sprouted everywhere to continue the human connection and communication. Digital volunteerism exploded. The Good Samaritans in Thailand set up a 'community cupboard' for food donations to hungry people. It continues to operate a suicide-prevention hotline since its inception in 1997. Not surprisingly, calls have increased dramatically since the onset of the virus. From these groups arose initiatives that extended assistance, both financial and non-financial, to needy family members and friends, with the understanding that repayment may not be forthcoming.

A force of 20,000 Kazakhs volunteered to distribute food and information about hygiene to rural Kazakhstan. In neighbouring Kyrgyzstan and Moldova, volunteers provided counselling support to affected populations under the aegis of Dmitry Frischin, regional manager of the UN Volunteer Office for Europe and Central Asia. The use of communications technology facilitated volunteers in Uzbekistan to contact people daily to provide care and counselling and even legal service. When the pandemic struck, the volunteers somehow emerged out of the woodwork all over the world. Surprisingly, there were so many of them, a quiet force ready to be mobilized without thought of monetary consideration or career enhancement.

We give out of a sense of Smithian sympathy and compassion, even while we also inhabit the world of economic competition. We are both self- *and* other-centred. Both parts of us are not always in perfect balance: one probably more pronounced than the other. But there is one certainty despite these tensions within: we exercise solidarity to collectively ensure our survival. This pandemic has taught us who we are, who we can be, even while these tensions within us continue. These are our human struggles. Already, this is a profound lesson that COVID continues to teach us.

I am still trying to meet Ray Lee Sheng, the Singaporean entrepreneur. While waiting in 2020, I studied the Samaritans, an ancient community of Jews of Samaria, now nearly extinct. This community was first encountered in the Gospel of Luke, chapter 10, verses 27–37, in which Jesus tells the parable of a Jew who was beaten and left on the side on the road. No one stopped by to help him except a Samaritan. The parable is exemplary in its simplicity: kindness can be shown towards a group to which he doesn't belong, in this case, a Samaritan towards a Levite (Jew).

When COVID shut down his noodle stall, the Samaritan story immediately came to my mind. It must have been that it was Easter Sunday or thereabouts when I read the story in my hospital bed. The parallelism of being sick, perhaps potentially mortally ill, was not lost on me. And so, I grasped this story as a window into my future, should I survive COVID. I wanted to know more about what Ray Lee Sheng is like.

I have no clue as to Ray's perspective of the world. Nor do I have any idea of the process that led him to decide, rather quickly, that he wanted to serve breakfast noodles to the elderly during the lockdown period in Singapore. I am still chasing him for an interview, but he has been very busy since the reopening of his stall as a business enterprise in mid-2020. He continues to distribute 100 packets of noodles daily to the homes of the elderly and the vulnerable. He hasn't abandoned his giving and feeding project. When I read about him while I was in the hospital, I was determined to meet him. A mere Facebook video simply won't do. I am also convinced that should another pandemic occur, Ray Lee Sheng will once again be at the frontlines of volunteerism, ready with his army of noodle-packet distributors. Having fully recovered, I have time to wait for Ray Lee Sheng. I have waited long enough. It will be worth it.

Chapter 7

How Do I Disrupt Thee? Let Me
Count the Ways

In between bites of roasted lamb, Fernando (not his real name) spoke to his wife on his mobile phone. He pleaded, entreated, beseeched, implored, appealed, adjured, cajoled, begged, argued, debated, invoked, petitioned, scolded. Finally, he just exploded with all his Mediterranean exasperation: get out of Italy and return to Shanghai with their son, Felipe (not his real name), while the borders were still open! His wife, Isabella (nor hers), an Italian of Chinese descent, got caught in Italy in late March 2020, just as the virus was roaring across the country on its first wave of infection. You get the drift.

Lunch was a sumptuous leg of lamb roast that I prepared meticulously for Fernando who came for the first time to our home since he arrived in Singapore in late 2019; a kind of welcome to a friend and colleague who managed to make a career shift out of Shanghai where he had lived and worked for over two decades. This was a momentous break for Fernando. He had taken the fork in the road and was happily re-settling in his new flat in Singapore. That is, until COVID.

Lunch ended. He hurriedly left and apologetically explained that the battle to get tickets had just been waged. The next forty-eight hours were crucial: he would have to monitor every minute and every hour of their journey from the moment they boarded the plane until they landed in Shanghai.

The next day, we heard from Fernando and learnt that Isabella and son, Felipe, were on the last flight out of Rome on a transit flight to Amsterdam, finally landing in Shanghai twenty-four hours later. A photo of her on the plane, fully masked, was final proof of life. She was truly on board. A belated thanks for the roast lamb.

Fernando had not slept in three days, he reported. Relieved, he hung up, and then he crashed.

Waking up the following morning, the next battle was about to be waged: what to do with their daughter Inez who was living and studying in Canterbury. Spring break was coming up and she was all by herself. Another long series of phone calls between Singapore and the UK ensued, calling friends to take in Inez (also not her real name) for the duration of the Spring break as her school had closed down. Another three days of sleeplessness. The bags under his eyes were purple and enlarged. His ears were burning with prolonged mobile-phone hours. He was losing more hair by the day. He finally succeeded in getting her to Singapore through multiple twists and turns with ticketing, bookings, reservations, visa applications. Inez stayed with Fernando for another four months until she returned to the UK for the Fall term.

For a short while, Fernando enjoyed some stability. His immediate family was in only two places rather than being scattered about all over the planet. Mother and son were in Shanghai; father and daughter in Singapore. His mother and grandmother and all his in-laws were in Italy, all of them in lockdown. No one was on the move; everyone was in place.

Disruption, to say the least, is the most (over)used term in 2020. The other is lockdown. Both words have crept very quickly into our vocabulary in record time. If one were to monitor thirty-minute conversations across the globe, these two words will certainly be uttered within the first ten minutes, max.

More than just speaking about it, however, is the steady incorporation of disruption into our lives. We've been at this for a year now, and we've even celebrated, nay remembered and commemorated, the first-ever coronavirus visit into our country. Daily, we monitored the infection rates and active cases. We followed the news and the rumours, we sifted fact from hearsay. By and large, we complied with lockdown measures even while a few others tried to defy, circumvent, thwart and resist them.

Before coronavirus, however, disruption was already on the horizon. Joseph Schumpeter, the eminent Austrian political economist, already spoke about 'creative destruction' as early as the 1940s to refer to innovations in the economic processes that raised productivity, particularly manufacturing output. The assembly line replaced prior processes, for example, artisanal production and craftwork. The automobile and steam locomotive replaced the horse-drawn carriage. In turn, the bullet train displaced the steam train. Soon, we will be riding driverless buses, taxis, cars.

On 29 January 1886, Carl Benz received patent number 37435 in recognition of the first automobile powered by a gas engine which he built. The patent is considered as the 'birth certificate' of the automobile. Since then, the automobile has morphed into several iterations, the latest of which is a hybrid model powered by both electricity and gas. Steam trains today are artifacts, resurrected from the past for nostalgic rides; for example, in Japan and the UK where supposedly there is a devoted following among passengers who are 'exhilarated by the sound, smell, and pace of steam', so wrote Simon Jenkins of the *Guardian*.

That was two centuries ago. We now take for granted the elevator, even though we do miss the uniformed elevator operators who pressed the buttons to go up and down the building. Who remembers the voluminous Britannica encyclopaedia these days, the cassette recorder, the personal travel agent, or the jalopy-driving music teacher who paid weekly visits to her students to dispense piano and flute lessons? We may still keep a library, but the Kindle that drops neatly into our handbags could very well hold all of our books, our journals, our newspapers and magazines and even our encyclopaedia.

But the disruption of the pandemic was of a specific kind. Rather than hasten our proficiency at daily life through the convenience of machine-dispensed services, COVID suddenly halted our long-cherished habits which, up until the outbreak, we had taken for granted. We haven't experienced rush hour in at least a year, sampled a buffet, hosted a mega-party, browsed in a bookstore, watched a movie, hung out with friends at a bar, danced in a night club, travelled on a food-binging impulse. Rather, we have been holed up at home, tentatively stepping outside with mask-covered faces. If you live in the Philippines, you were also required by law to wear a face shield over your mask. Having taken to the habit, many Filipinos have included alcohol and hand-sanitizers in their pockets, Betadine nasal sprays and throat gargles, even disposable gloves.

Disruption in our personal lives is not as easy as leading the thirsty horse to the water. Humans are creatures of habit, claims Kate Murphy of the *New York Times*. When routines are disrupted, the brain sends off signals that there is a disconnect between expectations and reality. Then distress sets in. It can be as simple as letting go of your most comfortable worn-out shoes or as wrenching as the sudden loss of your home to a fire or a flood. As humans, we are 'biologically engineered to get upset' when these regularities are gone. And so, we whine, complain, and when it gets unnerving, like imposed curfew, we rant, rave, protest, mindless about the danger of these super-spreading events.

Particularly disruptive was Christmas Eve and the traditional Noche Buena on 24 December which we celebrated every year with our mother living in Manila. For the last thirty years, between August and September, the siblings all over the world would start scouting for air tickets and airline routes that would ensure our arrival in time for the much-cherished Christmas Eve meal. Coordination of pick-up schedules at Manila's hysterical international airport during the Christmas season was a yearly exercise that became routinized with years of practice. With the discussions over email and Skype, the individual contributions to the meal were discussed, debated and finalized. Freshly baked *pan de sal* to match with honey ham and sharp Spanish *queso de bola* were indispensable. Champagne was obligatory even if none of us were fond of liquor. Sitting around our assigned seats at the massive square table that was a fixture in our ancestral home, we would all be sated and saturated until past midnight, and then we would turn our attention to the distribution of gifts. The ritual that has lasted for far too long was suddenly gone in 2020.

Instead, our phones, iPads, and laptops were on, all of them positioned on the dining table. It was a very awkward coordination of time zones. Manila and Singapore were having dinner while my siblings in Brussels, New York and California were either on breakfast or lunch time. At the stroke of midnight in Asia, we shrieked and screamed Happy New Year to drown the sorrow of separation. Meanwhile, New York had a long thirteen-hour wait until 2020 was firmly ejected, and California had to endure an additional three hours to finally bid the year goodbye.

It must have been true the world over: the digital celebration of the passing of a God-awful year, and the arrival of a new decade. Nobody liked it I am sure. But we all did it anyway. My brother had four Zoom celebrations spread throughout New Year's Eve across the world that never seemed to end. He complained, light-heartedly, that he had raised and clinked his champagne glass far too many times to remember in what time zone he was celebrating.

The funny thing is, however much we hated, even resisted disruptions, we ultimately succumbed to them. Selectively. But the selectivity sprang from a recognition that while this virus was having its field day feasting on our bodily proteins, we armed ourselves against its predatoriness. In the process, we made the adjustments so that we can practise the rituals that sustain us and keep us connected.

Disruption is creative. How else did we get from horse-drawn carriage to driverless bus? Stories of converted gardeners and cooks abound. Suddenly the pandemic produced aspiring chefs, novelists, poets, painters, interior decorators, landscape artists. I've returned to colouring books, branching out into *batik* designs, Japanese kimonos and Greek and Celtic mandalas. In our expansive estate of several condominiums, I've noticed balconies hosting multi-coloured orchids, graceful anthuriums, and creeping philodendrons twirling around the iron railings. Neighbours linger longer for morning coffee; hands wave to each other; smiling eyes are noticeably exchanged among masked passers-by. Birds have come to shelter themselves during a downpour or build nests in towering bamboo trees.

The hated mask that blocks airflow from our nostrils has now undergone several redesigns—upgraded versions from the lowly three-ply mask that looked like folded paper napkins slapped across one's face.

My favourite version is a K95 mask made of five layers, snugly outfitted into a silicone case with a large filter element and breathing valve, allowing the mask to sit a few centimetres away from my nose. It covers my face entirely, albeit fashionably. The space in between the case and my nose lets a smooth inflow and outflow of air. My nose doesn't feel it's been quashed, nor do I feel suffocated. Plus, it has a shiny exterior, giving off a chic look.

The final piece of ingenuity are the adjustable straps that hold the mask firmly in place. The straps run throughout the silicone casing past my ears to the back of my neck where I firmly pull the straps that are held together by a stopper and adjust accordingly. Best of all, the filters are replaceable and washable. And the casing comes in three colours: soft grey, straightforward black and baby blue. No sweat. Why should we all look monochromatic?

Returning to our friend, Fernando, over a year has passed since he arrived in Singapore. He has taken to a new routine that was totally different from what he imagined before the pandemic. If all went according to plan, his wife and son would have joined him in Singapore, or he would have made the relatively short trips to Shanghai for quick and easy visits. And his daughter would join them during her school holidays. The global family pattern had its well-established routines.

But the pandemic upended all the best, well-laid plans. He hasn't seen his wife and son for almost two years. His daughter in the UK is in a tier-four zone with very stringent measures. She may not be able to come to Singapore for a while given the anxiety over Omicron. His grandmother in Italy passed away from COVID in early January 2021. We have a photo of her sent through the mobile phone, sitting serenely during what must have been her final days. And then a second photo of a casket being brought into a small church for a hasty funeral. His mother is alone.

He is distraught. And all alone.

But he soldiers on bravely. Thanks to a kitchen robot that he imported from Switzerland he manages to prepare meals to perfection. I've tasted the best hummus from his machine—creamy, smooth, perfectly blended. The home-made pasta is man and machine-made. And his floors are swept by a robot vacuum cleaner that knows where the electrical outlet is located to recharge itself.

He has video games that transport him to a virtual war zone where he fends off attacks, protects borders, vanquishes enemies through alliances with virtual warriors. He has reconstructed his life with large, built-in, virtual components.

Throughout these many months of the pandemic, I am emotionally exhausted at what Fernando had to live through and continues to. His latest effort is to get a vaccine so that he can travel to Italy and finally visit his mother. Thus far, he has succeeded to get in front of the vaccine queue on grounds of a family emergency. His rebooked ticket many times over is an unfailing effort to give himself a respite from what has been a year of never-ending readjustments.

After what seemed an eternity, Fernando boarded a midnight plane to Italy in late April 2021. But not after badgering several clinics in Singapore to give him his two vaccinations. He sent me several text messages on his way to the airport. Quite discordant, still in disbelief that the journey was finally happening. Arrived in Turin, straight into quarantine. It would be weeks before he would actually see his mother. But the long dreadful wait to see her was over. It was the first taste of home.

And the subsequent days spent meeting with friends and family was as if all that struggle mattered little. I received uploaded photos in WhatsApp of glorious Italian cuisine that he succumbed to every single day in Italy. He spoke nothing about weight gain, and I wasn't allowed to mention calories. There were long walks and drives with his mother. His daughter came over from the UK for a summer visit. For him, it almost felt like completion. The last hurdle was to visit his wife and son in Shanghai.

Four months later, he returned to Singapore. After the mandatory fourteen-day quarantine, he was at our home, armed with pesto and Italian wine. He is refreshed from the trip and time with his mother was like spiritual upliftment. Who knows when he can see her again, given another round of outbreaks in Europe?

But his preoccupation since his arrival is to be present as his son's forthcoming eighteenth birthday in 2022. It will be two years since he had seen him and his wife. The disruption continues. Fernando soldiers on. For the past twenty-four months, he lived through multiple disruptions. But like millions of others, he finds within himself the resources to live through another day. Sometimes with grace, other times with humour, but always with strength and determination. On other days, he sounds like he wants to lose it. But he restrains himself. He wants to continue living as we all do. As we all want to do. As we all definitely will.

Chapter 8

Remembrances of Sleazy Street

I miss Bangkok—its funny mixing and melding of chaos and order, of Buddhist repose and urban loudness, its pleasurable incoherence. Bangkok is not reducible to a single adjective as other cities are. Like smart Singapore, quaint Boston, chic Paris, dusty Khartoum, nostalgic San Francisco, exotic Vientiane, hyper-diverse Montreal, solemn Jerusalem, mysterious Thimphu.

Soi 4 is a shortcut. Interpret that in at least two ways: a way of avoiding the afternoon traffic on Sukhumvit Road, Bangkok's main thoroughfare; or as a visual quickie, a shortcut to instant titillation. Interestingly, you can combine both in one sitting: avoid the traffic altogether while having a lascivious treat from your car window.

On the south side of this short road are medium-rise residential condos, many of them walled in by concrete fences and a thin strip of greenery. The flats are lined up so close together one could look out into each other's living rooms. An occasional indoor flowerpot or bamboo shade mutes the slouching neighbour in front of his TV, while the traipsing lady in her early evening pyjamas serves as the only hindrance to an uninterrupted view of Thai domesticity.

On the north side is a luggage shop, across from a 7–11 convenience store. Noodle hawkers crowd each other out on the pavements, just enough space for these motorized *tuktuks* to squeeze through without knocking down glass-encased roasted ducks hanging dead by their beaks.

Soi 4 is narrow and noisy, a navigational impediment meant only for the veteran driver. It becomes naughty at night, increasingly so as the night wears on. A paradise for perverts. Like Sodom and Gomorrah in the middle of Bethlehem, this mini, red-light district is charming if only because it is so incongruously planted in an otherwise respectable neighbourhood.

Bars and women and farangs everywhere, in all stages of dress and undress. Belly buttons exposed; low-cut blouses with cleavages staring in your face; shoulders and arms outstretched to reach into your intimate parts; hips swaying on a humid afternoon; thighs and legs wrapped in fishnet stockings; red, platform heels; earrings dangling on painful earlobes, thick facial make-up to provide comfort in anonymity. Men in a state of utter disrepair as they fondled the women's fronts, backs, behinds—in full public view of every passer-by.

On an early afternoon, some of the women who had not lucked on a customer stood close to the centre of the street with numerous body parts laid out suggestively, in a bodily plea to take them for Happy Hour, so that he may have a happy ending.

Just my luck. Arriving from a weekend trip from southern China in mid-2004, I hoped to reach home before sin street opened for business. Thus, the shortcut route. Nope. I ended up stuck in the middle of perverts-in-progress.

The taxi driver decided it was time for a conversation, how else to sit it out in a traffic jam? 'Sek, sek, sek here, all the time, e-ve-ly day. E-ve-ly body make love if you like watch.' The charm of Thai language is what's missing: the letters 'x' and 'r.'

'Are you propositioning me?' I thought to ask him, then dropped it. It's too much work, too complicated. Homeward bound, however laborious this was proving to be, was top priority.

That was over a decade ago. This need to remember and revisit, I attribute to lockdown, travel ban and the longing for mobility. I yearned to move around and explore, flex my curiosity muscles, drink in the massive outdoor entertainment that we're all missing at home. Without facial masks, without fear. With thoughts of a virus still on the loose, I re-entered Soi 4 through the best available means—via YouTube. Welcome to the world of digital tourism.

It is an early evening in August 2020. It is the height of Thailand's lockdown to the outside world. Borders have been practically closed. The tourists have all but disappeared from the Thai landscape. No one leaves the kingdom, very few enter. To peek into the country, set up your laptop, click on the YouTube app.

An intrepid vlogger codenamed TravelMate rode his motorcycle and strapped a smartphone on the handles of his vehicle. I imagine that's what he did to capture the scenery live.

He led us into electronic Soi 4, entered through the north side coming from Sukhumvit the main road after a lengthy detour from opposite Soi 11. Lo and behold, the luggage shop was still there with an additional rack of umbrellas parked right on the sidewalk. Across the alley was a row of motorcycle taxis all at a standstill, like an army waiting for a skirmish. There were no passengers to ferry. Where once I sat in an immovable traffic jam fifteen years ago, Soi 4 during the pandemic was a two-way lane with no movement anywhere.

A little further into the street were the long-legged vamps in platform heels. Those massive encasements could kill you with just one kick. One wore a leather mini-skirt and a black-bra top. Another donned a long wrap-around sarong also with a black-bra top, and still another, a short loose skirt that twirled around her waist as she pivoted to some pulsating music, revealing her black underwear. Black must be the name of the evening game. They posed for the camera, they're playful. Business was much slower than it ever was, but they were determined to have fun in this otherwise virus-victimized alley.

TravelMate continued to cruise. He captured the boarded-up bars and restaurants that were, not too long ago, vibrant and over-crowded. Stumble Inn remained open, but I imagine there wasn't too much stumbling going on inside. Staff loitered around waiting for customers to come. Few people walked past. Hooters, the icon of titillation, was empty. A solitary bosomy waitress, Hooters signature brand, promenaded slowly across the floor, hoping for more action. Thus far, the action was all of her impatiently pacing to and fro. Another long, slow night. No one was interested in a generous helping of Hooters burger and fries with the bosomy bonus that came with the service, free of charge.

Still further is Nana Plaza, a down-market emporium of goods that ranged from leopard-skin-print T-shirts to spandex tank-tops. Approximately thirty neon bulbs shone their light on three persons at the entrance. They glowered in the emptiness. A bored storekeeper served as a foreground to a dazzling array of scarves, all of diverse lengths, shades and colours. Some are for your head and neck; others to dangle on your shoulders; many to wear as a facial mask in an attempt at fashionable reinvention of mandated pandemic gear. There were so few buyers, and the display items seemed fossilized for months.

TravelMate captured a few more familiar scenes. The noodle-soup vendor's cart was ubiquitous, even for a solitary customer enjoying an early evening slurp. On the opposite side of the alley was the Tattoo-and-Piercing shop, whose main attraction was the outstretched thigh of a woman sitting on a high chair, her other leg dangling aimlessly as she awaited customers who don't seem to have the stamina for an ink-and-needle job while a virus was on the loose. A flaming-red billboard up ahead broadcasted Leo soda water in a frosted white bottle engraved with a lion's image. The legend above the bottle cap read, 'A World of Fun.'

Bangkok is all of a wondrous city of canals and patios, flame trees and sidewalk markets, rumbling *tuktuks* (motorized two-seater vehicles with side cars) and pink taxis. Gold and jade, silk and linen, willow trees and lagoons. Spirit houses are adorned with incense, candles and ribbons to appease the spirits and shelter them when they need rest. And of course, food that is worthy of a culinary orgy. Lemongrass, lemon and lime, ginger, turmeric and galangal, on fish, fowl, rice, bread and grain—you only, and always, want to gorge.

But it is also very much like the 2008 film *Bangkok Dangerous* starring Nicolas Cage. A cold-blooded assassin, a corrupt client, a martial-arts-savvy sidekick, a ruthless, crazed villain, a gorgeous chick—all of them sort of jumbled together in a hodgepodge plot of violence, fast-paced action, choreographed fight scenes and tender seductive moments in a pharmacy. Both hero and heroine hold hands in luminous Lumpini Park while behind them, a robbery is in full swing and a guy gets stabbed for a few bills of Thai baht from his wallet. Blood splatters across the screen while Nicolas Cage's face is contorted with pangs of guilt and pain, trying to decide whether to elope with this gentle gazelle he met at the cash register, or lop off the villain's head as a worthy rival to Marlon Brando's decapitation in *Apocalypse Now*. The movie ends without firm resolution. Our anti-hero escapes a bomb blast in his home by crouching in the bathtub. The villain in pursuit may still be alive. One can't decide if this flick was Asia's response to *Pulp Fiction*. One can't decide if Bangkok is really dangerous or just downright discursive.

I used to live in the neighbourhood of Soi 4 in 2004. The entrance to the condominium was non-descript. No fancy lobby with marble floors or long impressive driveways. No smart receptionist in stiletto heels. Only an abrupt entrance to narrow carparks and a sweet, blue-shirted sentry standing at attention whenever anyone arrived, otherwise slouched all day in a rather cramped outpost. He would always meet me every time I returned from travel. For fifty Thai baht, the equivalent of almost $2, he would haul up my suitcase and fold his hands in the traditional *wai* greeting as he walked down with his measly stash that would buy him a skewer of fried fish balls or a bowl of noodles at the corner. His smile was always melting: two missing front teeth that would cast away fatigue and scepticism from the most hardened traveller.

Right next to the sentry's outpost is the spirit house, always adorned and fancily bedecked with fresh marigolds, incense, bottled water and food to appease the spirit wanderers. Sentry and spirit both, they protected me, and I slept deeply, even with the sound of cackling geckos somewhere in the ceiling of my bedroom.

Hidden cameras hung on trees to protect the US embassy staff residences that were directly opposite my flat. The cameras that were

installed for President George W. Bush's visit in 2003, were never
removed, say the Filipina maids of the embassy personnel. I watched
a diplomat run on his treadmill every afternoon, finishing with a towel
wipe-off and a good many drags on his cigarette right after the workout.
He watched me watching him. Maybe. The tall thick stalks of heliconias
in my front yard were not enough to conceal his incongruous habits. I
must have seemed to him like a green stalker. I relished this delightful
scenery of humans and their strange predilections on display. They
only happen in Bangkok.

In this neighbourhood was the relocated girly bars from the
Patpong district that gave the latter its merit of distinction in the 1970s.
Soi 4 sheltered them for at least half the street, while the other half
retained its bourgeois character of handsome, high-rise condos and
respectable, dining places. TravelMate Vlogger on his motorcycle had
approached the sober half of Soi 4, and it is an evening of creeping
darkness, made gentle by garden lights and bougainvillea trees in
full bloom while chauffeur-driven cars drop off their well-dressed
employers. The vibrating noise of the bars in the northern part of Soi
4 recedes. A quick turn and TravelMate has left Soi 4.

Digitally, we are within spitting distance of the US Embassy
compound. This contiguity, to be sure, didn't, and couldn't, prevent
anyone to break the diplomatic cordon of safety when the tug of
vice lures away the compound's inhabitants, even with the best
protective devices and surveillance gizmos. So did a friend of mine
who complained to me years ago. Her American diplomat husband
whose curiosity about the ongoings at nearby Soi 4 was a perpetual
point for conjugal discussions. If he wished to sneak out for a peek or
more, no hidden camera or over-protective wife can stop him. She set
her boundaries with him finally, to end all circuitous discussions that
would inevitably end at Soi 4. She established them firmly above the
region of his neck, not any further below.

'Think only, look only, do not do, do not touch, not ever,' she
commanded him with a hearty if not exasperated chuckle and a shrug
of her shoulders in surrender.

Under lockdown, I mused about life in South East Asia that cuts both ways: there are the sleazy parts like Soi 4, and there's the magnificence of the Emerald Buddha across the city, housed in a complex of temples known as Wat Phra Kaew. There's Soi Cowboy just a few blocks away from Soi 4, a kind of mirror image to each other. But there's the terrace at the Oriental Hotel which awarded the novelist Somerset Maugham an exquisite view of South East Asia for his inspired short stories about love, lust, betrayal, benevolence, kindness, cruelty.

There's neon-light rain with body-stockinged women in a gaudy bar, and there's the handsome proprietrix at the gorgeous tea shop, two blocks away, on Soi 8. She is immaculately dressed in flowing ecru palazzo pants and a white sleeveless top, generous with her wealth of Pu-erh tea, aged for fifty years.

She gave me a small canister to try, swore that the taste of ten-year Pu-erh will bite my taste buds, whereas fifty-year Pu-erh will massage them. She washed the tea leaves a few times, its dark brown-reddish water flowed into a tray with bamboo slats. The sting and sharpness of the first few leaves are removed from the water's steam and the heat. Her fingers wrapped around the teacup so delicately, like she was playing a harp. Then she commanded me to 'make cup disappear'. The heat enveloped my hand for a few solemn minutes. 'Then drink,' she said. Her voice was half laughter, half song. Truly, it was the grace of the ritual that glided on my taste buds. I couldn't really tell the difference between ten and fifty, as clueless as I am between single malts and blended Scotch. But the effect was divine: sampling tea in this manner before purchase seemed prayerful rather than transactional.

I pondered, as I sipped my fifty-year-old Pu-erh tea, the wickedly delicious irony of this unforgettable city. And I remember even more, this city of grace and gore, of brute force and gentle curves. As only a pandemic can cause us to remember.

Chapter 9

I Feel an Ache Today

Day fifteen in the hospital. Easter Sunday was yesterday. I couldn't hear the church bells. The double-glazed windows eradicated all the noise. Or perhaps, this is the sound of the pandemic. Complete and utter silence.

Too much time here, hours to wait for the doctor's next visit, the next swab-test results, the weekly delivery of fresh hospital-issued pyjamas, the planned meal. An excruciatingly long wait for this virus to finally tire of me and take leave, waiting to go home, rejoin the living and the healthy, be fully human again, COVID-free. That was when I thought of her.

I thought of how her life was of unremitting pain. Fifty years, longer maybe? Waiting for the pain to end. Watching, waiting, not knowing where the pain was in her body. How it comes, how long it stays, she never knows, never could.

I feel an ache today
Where is it this morning?
In my rheumatic knees?

In my belly, where a thick scar
Grew from surgery
Thirty years ago?
Or my left upper cheek
Where my eye tics
Faster when I am afraid

Maybe a stroke
Maybe I'm going blind
Maybe going insane
From the pain
From the pain
From the never-ending
Unstoppable pain

It sprang upon her like a thief in the night, interrupted her sleep, startled her, awakening her from the afternoon slumber attacked her at mid-morning when in the garden for fresh air, for small, studied walks with ailing knees, private musings, a moment's peace when he was not whining, complaining, glowering.

He suffered from weakened lungs, an accelerating emphysema due to years of heavy smoking. He succumbed to vicious asthma attacks at the slightest hint of rain or when the gardener trimmed the grass. His brother passed away from the same illness, two brothers with big voices, whose shouting could bring down the skies. They turned helpless, whimpering and despondent during horrible visits of asthma.

She built a grand house for him to recover from his weakened lungs or to feel relief from the emphysema. The carefully landscaped garden invited early morning birds to come sing for a few grains of rice. She was lost in the splendour of constructing the home that was her daily kingdom, where she reigned supreme. The workers did her bidding and she was gone for several hours a day, away from him for a while. When she returned, it started all over again . . . the coping, the caring, the managing. A woman's work never ends.

He snores loudly
He could burst my eardrums;
He inhaled thunder
And exhaled a raging wind
Like something stored for centuries
His furious breath expelled
Into my face
His mouth
Begins to murmur
Someone chases him in his sleep,
The rising crescendo of his snorting
Begins yet again

Such has been my nights
for fifty-three years.

Ah, to be eighty years old,
Is it your body,
or your heart
that hurts so
so very much?

I remembered the first complaints, so physical. At fifty years old, her ovaries were removed. Six children and eight pregnancies later, she felt her womanhood come to a crashing end. The hormones that lubricated her skin and hair had dried and dissipated, the hormones that gave her those bodily urges to have her husband stroke her, tease her, arouse her, keep her desirable. For twenty-five years, she was the sole focus of his love and lust . . . until the disappeared ovaries, her abandoned womb, her emptied womanhood.

Where is it in my body?
Sometimes
In my finger joints
Arthritic, crooked

Eating too many shrimps
And duck eggs,
Or even just
A mild dose of pork cracklings
I served the Mahjong guests
Yesterday

At the base of my nape
Pinching, twitching
From boiled pork
In sour broth and mustard leaves
Oily peanuts
Spicy, garlicky
Deadly

In a hospital faraway more than a decade ago, when my womanhood was at the brink, I waited to sign the medical papers. I was alone in this desolate room. It was a cold dreary night, the air conditioner hummed noisily, the sheets smelled of industrial detergent, the cotton blanket was frayed and thin.

He, the surgeon with a forgettable name, will cut me open first thing the next morning. My ovaries will be removed. There were fibroids the size of tennis balls in my right ovary, another bunch of grape-sized ones at the centre. A bountiful harvest of unnecessary growths. Just like her womb, her body, her womanhood.

My belly is flat, smooth, with taut skin. I am forty-seven years old. At the peak of my womanhood. The nurse came in late in the evening, shaved my pubic hair, prepared me for surgery. I wanted to scream from shock. I felt humiliated, enraged. A piece of my womanhood was being razored away.

Gone in an hour, from the surgeon's scalpel and experienced hands. I wondered, as she did, if I would ever be young again with oestrogen-fed skin. Or would my body, like hers, dry up like a hardened desiccated coconut.

Her body is bereft of desire. A keloidal scar takes its place above her pubic bone, where skin, hair and scar collide as though a cruel meeting on her body that she no longer knows, controls or recognizes. A hair follicle enlarges, expands, then turns into a boil. The pus bursts, oozes, pukes. A disgusting vomit. It stops, itches, crusts, dries, closes and heals. The hair grows and shoots out of the skin pore where the pus has left its ugly mark. The skin is quiet for a while, a short bodily peace, until the scar comes to life again. Like an eel crawling across her belly, getting thicker, bigger, angrier until her belly is nothing but a hideous, thick, brown-red crust.

For over thirty years, she endured this angry snake that wouldn't leave her, that awakens when the hair follicle grows when the pimple explodes, and her belly is a filthy mess of blood and pus.

She is bloated, her stomach distended. Too many pregnancies, too many foetuses formed in this small vessel, then disgorged into the world, crying, demanding. She fed them all, suckled them at her breast, grew them into human beings. Her body is tired, overused. Each birth, a reminder of the pain she endured.

I wake up,
My world spinning out of orbit
I slept so little

The television blared
until 4 a.m.
he switched it off
and I finally asleep

Then his mouth opens
Exhales
murmurs
louder
even louder
and again
and more

an invisible hand
clasps at his throat
only his will
to breathe
while asleep
and I know
he is still alive

Tomorrow I will be
Dizzy again
Lack of sleep
His loud breath
Very loud
In my right ear

Where the nerves
Are failing, feeling
Like they are
Falling
And I am also
Falling
And fading fast

And the room will
Move, shake and spin
Until it stops
And I will wait
Until it stops
If it stops

The wound in my belly mended. A small scar, a tiny worm ran down my mid-stomach. There was no reminder of the surgeon's scalpel. The acupuncturist pierced needles into the scar and killed the worm, blinded its eyes and punctured its head. Permanently. 'It won't ever bother you again,' she said.

There was no blood, no boil, no pus, no bursting pimple or blocked follicle. My worm was tamed early, then died when the acupuncture needles pricked the life out of this threatening scar. My belly is free from all growth, the skin is taut again, even if my womb is forever empty.

That was long ago.

I lay in this hospital, a different one in a different place and time, twenty-one years later. The temperature was cold and controlled. Good for my lungs, the fever was gone. I felt my body. My skin was parched dry, my limbs were cool, my hair unwashed for ten days. A sensor monitored my fever, undulating. I was never in mortal danger.

The taste of hydroxychloroquine lingered on my tongue, mingled with antihistamines and paracetamols. Steroidal puffs into my lungs opened air passageways. I felt the scars there thickening. They hurt. I had no desire for food or drink, only for this lethal virus to stop its battle with me.

I am sixty-nine years old. It was a long wait to my victory. I fought with all my remaining years, my body intact even without the ovaries, even with a dried-up scar in my belly. I waited and gathered my courage, my resoluteness to snatch my life swiftly, to regain my essence. I want to be, and I will be, whole again.

But she is all alone to bear her sorrows. From her belly, the worm is now in her knees. A short keloidal stump from another surgery a decade ago. She still wants to walk and not be confined in a wheelchair. She wants to stand, maybe move her hips a bit, swing them to light music, flail her arms in the air, laugh a little more. There have been too many years of harbouring pain and she is alone, all alone. That is the most bitter pain of all.

This morning
It is in my chest
I must breathe deeper,
Fill your lungs with air, the doctors say
I breathe deeply,
It is a heavy sigh
So I breathe lightly
So my heart can endure

He has gone
He has left
A farewell so unclear
So unsure
Like he would stay
But he didn't

He died
So quickly
and left me
Like Death stole him
Before he said goodbye

I am hurt
I bleed
I weep
I am alone
I am so alone
I am all so very much alone

At the taxi stand that would take me home, I clung to the potted plant to keep from passing out. I was almost without breath. The short walk to the hospital entrance left me gasping. I have just started recovering from this vicious virus.

The pain of waiting ended. It wasn't long after all: twenty-five hospital days. Not twenty-five years, like her waiting. Mine ended, hers didn't. My enemy was a virus, vicious and unseen. I outran this virus. I have patience, I have determination, I can and have endured.

Unlike her years of waiting in the dark, hoping that he will maybe return. Even if only to say goodbye properly, tenderly. To ask for forgiveness. To forgive him. To remember the years of love and joy, when they were younger and full of vigour. When he was foolishly in love with her, only eyes for her.

He didn't hold her, he didn't touch her, he didn't shed a tear, he didn't give her a tender farewell, a moment of gratitude for all those years, those many tormented, tedious, terrific, troublesome, traumatic, tremendous, tender, titanic years. He breathed his last, and she was unprepared. Not even a chance to hold his hand and touch his face again. He gasped one last time and lifted himself out of his long-tormented body.

He died leaving her a broken woman. Her years are spent in regret. Her youthful years of mishaps, mistakes and misunderstandings. She eloped, married and regretted every single day. She should have said no, should have gone home. She should have listened to the berating of her father and the wailing of her mother, the castigated pleas of her brothers, the cajoling of her cousins and the ridicule of her in-laws.

All of them she tried to please, but now that they are all gone, she has not pleased herself for one moment. Her life was spent for others, wasted.

The bad memories won't go away. The dank dark church and the bored priest who pronounced her a wife in the sordid dusk hour when she was unsure that this was the man she was committed to for life.

Then anger, red, hot, flaming, furious anger, over her mistakes, her stupid mistakes, her past that can't be recovered. All that loss. Irretrievable. The years pass one into the other. The winter of her life has come. Still, she finds her mind unable to forget. And forgive.

Should I have left?
Where would I have gone?

A woman without hormones
With flawed skin
And drooping eyes
Sagging mouth
Wrinkled jaw
Where could an old woman go?

Without my knees
I cannot even walk
Without my courage

I cannot walk away
Without my freedom
I am stuck
And stumped

I arrive home, the fragrance of fresh flowers burst into my nostrils. Melted cheese pizzas and barbecued chicken wings greet me with jubilation. I have been starving for twenty-five days.

He hugs my emaciated frame so tightly my shoulder joints crack. We both laugh. I live again, I eat again, I couldn't stop eating. Every taste bud has reawakened. I burp and belch. The enzymes gurgle, breaking down the sinful chocolates, heavy protein, thick fibre, unhealthy carbohydrates. My shrunken belly began to expand. My cheeks filled out, my face lifted. My bluish lips turned crimson again. I filled out my clothes. I don't care about vanity. I have left the Valley of Death.

My beloved stayed and waited. Twenty-five days of longing. Free, full, fearless. Without compromise, without hesitation. Openly loving in the bright sun, the wide world to watch and wonder. To ponder each other's mysteries. A lifetime ahead to feel tenderness, exchange kindness, trust, respect, renew and resurrect. Love can never be, should never be, a lesser bargain.

She receded into memory, but her pains still haunt me. After COVID, when I have mild headaches, aching joints, feverish feet, sneezing and sniffling, gasping for air upon sudden movements, she returns to my thoughts. How she continues to endure, afraid of other pains that will add to those she already has, feeling mortality every single day. Without him. Without us. Without me. It is the pain of being so mortally alone.

Should I take my medicine?
Perhaps it is arthritis
After all
I feel it in
My knee joint
Valium tonight

To help me sleep
To ease the pain
While asleep
Until the morning
When the pains return
Yet again

I will call the doctor,
think about Mahjong today.

When I wake up,
My ache will
Have disappeared.

Maybe
For a while
Even
For just
A little while

Chapter 10

Letters to/from my Dead Father

Dear Dad,

Where are you now? You've been gone so long. Is it nineteen, or twenty years? Has it been almost two decades? Somehow the years fold into each other.

It must be because my hair is full of grey now. The bags beneath my eyes are bigger, my waist is thicker and my hair is thinner. You have been gone so long.

I am starting to forget things. I misread texts—yes, those mysterious words that come out of a hand-held phone. You barely knew what they were two decades ago. You were surprised about emails. And no one wanted to teach you how to write them. So, you asked your eleven-year-old grandson. Niko taught you patiently, and in about four hours, you wrote to all of us. You didn't stop. You had found a new toy. A new monster, your oldest son said. We laughed, we read your emails, we answered. Immediately. Judiciously. We knew you didn't have too much time.

In which side of the universe are you hiding? Which stars keep you hidden? Which planets revolve around our world that keep your existence after your physical death?

Where are you, my children? It is turning dark and my world is dimming. There is so much I need to tell all of you, things to do that should not remain unfixed. My breath is shortening, and the phlegm thickens, slowly overtaking my lungs. My belly is weak, and I am hungry. Hungry for your presence, all six of you.

A needle is stuck in my veins and my arm hurts. Still, I write to all of you. Because you are bigger than all my pain, you light my world as it dims. You all help me fight the creeping darkness.

I monitor all your flights. It must have been eight hours since you all left Boston and San Francisco. My patience does not seem to wither. I only wish this waiting would not consume me.

I am driven by the fire to live because you are all so grown, and you have become magnificent adults. There is so little time and I wish to be given more, a little more. For you to lie next to me, to warm my cold hospital bed. Then I should have eaten, and my soul will be fed and full.

A very long cough. A very short breath. The cough stays, the breath leaves. You would put your arm on the table and force the cough out of your lungs so that the phlegm would loosen and you could breathe again. Evenings were long and dinner was often a non-stop fit of hacking. We watched you, and heard you, and watched and waited for those very long moments for your breath to return.

You went away so suddenly, that's how it felt, even if we all knew that you were sick for a long time. Your coughing ceased. Your breathing was thin over the telephone as I said my goodbye. You wouldn't reply, you couldn't. The longest moment when your life, and your breath, slipped into that place I know not where.

We named you Ramon, my oldest son, the favoured name of that era, signifying a nobility that harks back from ancient Spain. We named you for the first of all the grandsons.

You have to be stout-hearted and stately, I told him once, when I was close to leaving. You should have to be at the helm of our expanding clan. You must take over from me, you must be better than me. But I did not leave, not that time. But he took over and took charge. He is everyone's *Kuya*, the oldest of them all, to be revered and obeyed, to dispense counsel and advice, to show equanimity and fairness.

I remember his appetite. He eats for volume. His stomach was a bottomless and insatiable canister of hunger. At Redondo Beach in Los Angeles many years ago, we bought a bucket of crabs, clams, mussels and oysters. We spent the afternoon eating. I watched him gorge and pick away at the sinews and claws of those helpless crustaceans. When he gulped down the last of the lemon-shucked oyster, he beamed and thought of the Chinese buffet in the evening. No, he would never back away from an eating bout. For sure, he did not inherit my eating genes, because I am prone to boiled, broiled and grilled cuisine—the kind that would only entice him during the fasting season of Lent.

He is mostly joyful, and the motto of his life must have been: if in doubt, crack a joke. His humour saves us all from the tensions of every day and there is none too serious that he cannot convert into a witticism. His laughter is his most precious legacy to his own firstborn son who has inherited the gift of his cheerfulness. His anger is slow and rare, and when it does arrive at the doorstep of his being, it is a quiet explosion, like the proverbial sound of a falling leaf. No, he is not like me with my thunderous temper. His soft-spoken manner counters my voice that could blast away the closed windows of our home. How fortuitous that I should bear the oldest son with a gentle voice and a rapacious appetite!

Ramon still cannot talk about you. It's twenty years later. Once, on our Sunday Zoom calls, he asked, 'Are we still in mourning?' And then he stopped, and we were all silent. It was both a question and a statement.

Why is he still so sorrowful, I wonder? Is it the responsibility of being the oldest son and grandson, on both sides of his lineage? Is it the burden of family secrets that he must protect? An image of you that he must uphold?

He is a big eater. Still. That has not changed. No buffet is too large and he will not back away from a challenge. He will eat us all under the table, from one meal to the next. Food and humour sustain him. Yes, he would rather eat than be angry. He would choose sushi and tiramisu over a temper tantrum. He is unlike you in that way, Dad.

But he hides his sorrow behind the food. The dining table is the place where he can deflect all his emotions. Chew, munch and forget. Better to ingest calories than confront conundrums. It must be his scourge and his privilege all at once—to carry and command responsibility for being the eldest, and to carry that perpetual burden.

The youngest one, Jose Isidro Benjamin, we named you after me and the Catholic saint of the day on which you were born. I remember how, in your earliest days, you dissected your food like a scientist in a laboratory. Watched each molecule move before you put a small piece of fish in your delicate mouth. So unlike Ramon, with the perpetually hungry belly.

Josefina, my youngest daughter, named again after myself, as though that would ensure my immortality. Thereafter, she was called Joyce, and indeed, all the happiness that came with her sudden arrival into our family of six, she embodied. I threw a magnificent party when she was baptized because I wanted to honour the impossible. She was born at the exact noon hour in the tiny northern city of fragrant pine trees and hillside summer homes. It was then on an exuberant March day that she spewed forth her first cry, and my heart must have exploded. She was alive and I, more so.

You were both pre-teen enemies. You scratched and screeched at each other. Your quarrels amused me. You now remember your silly feuds—the drowning of the poor pet turtle and your sister's long nails that peeled your skin, the chocolate smudges on her mouth, the dried mangos hidden in your closet. I wondered if I should summon another Solomonic pronouncement to end this row.

But such are your childish ways. Your dislikes are stronger for reasons that are so insane. You resume them in jest as if to recover your lost innocence. Whereas I remember only that you were my two children, given to me during my advancing years. How youthful I felt again when you two, small precious infants with tiny hands, clutched my stout fingers and touched my heart.

Yes, Dad, they've stopped fighting and feuding. So many of those quarrels we mediated and interfered like homegrown referees. We were their surrogate parents: older children who shared parenting with you and Mom. When they stopped, it was like the last wave hitting the shore at midnight. Jose finally surpassed Joyce in height, and he was relieved. Youngest though he may be, he will tower above her, and lay final claim to his authority that being taller than she was all he needed to prove his worth.

You watched Joyce depart for Europe one unsuspecting day some forty years ago when she was in her tender twenties. None of it you truly understood. 'Why Belgium?', you asked. There was no one there, no one to look after her? You had all these fatherly questions, fears of a parent stoked with age and the loneliness of losing your children to adulthood.

She looked so determined to go. How does one stop an irrepressible spirit? It was, after all, your admonition, to go into the world and make something more of ourselves. To sever the ties to our mother's apron strings, you said, and make the world our home.

'Live an interesting life. It's easy to be ordinary,' you once said. She remembered your wise words.

When she boarded the plane, you were proud and anxious. Your little joy, now a grown woman, had gone forth to conquer a piece of the world, and herself as well. You let her go. Yet she would return even more often, as if she never left. She was there until your very last breath.

Cynthia, so much like your name, is an exuberant flower whose petals bud only in May. That was the month you were born. Your hands are like candles, your skin is alabaster. Your mother's jewellery always looked best on you. But your eyes. They are perennially sad. I often wondered if it was the sadness of the oldest daughter who must handle the burdens of everybody else, who must care for others and forget your own exhaustion.

You learned so early to concoct the family meals, track the household resources, navigate the morning markets on Sunday mornings after church. When the meat and fish stalls opened, you were ready with your shopping bags and your willingness to bargain. You came home, bursting with good intentions to fix the family breakfast, and you dispatched the household servants about their duties. At ten years of age, you knew how to change the diapers of Jose and warm the milk bottle of Joyce, both of them still infants, barely out of their mother's womb.

You took charge as the she-captain of the family home. My delicate flower is a wilful homemaker, even as you manoeuvre the labyrinths of the stock market and negotiate the legal contracts of your company. No wonder your eyes droop so often. You are working everywhere you go. For you, working is a compulsion.

Yes, Dad, your oldest daughter is a delight to us too, all her siblings. She is sturdy as a boulder, gentle as evening rain. Her tenderness must have come from Carla, a specially gifted child with equally beautiful skin like her mother's, black hair thick as an undisturbed forest. She was born with the burden of immovable limbs and her world is confined to a wheelchair. She hears the sounds of some faraway universe and maybe she sees the dance of the angels and the glow of their auras. She penetrates another life only she can know because she cannot speak. Maybe it is Carla who can see you in another galaxy because both of you are no longer in this world.

Cynthia got sick with COVID over Christmas in 2020, just as we all thought the year would end on a better note. They all did— her husband, her caregiver and Carla too. We were all so frightened, nervous discussions on WhatsApp twice a day, once every evening. Their daily temperature reports, oxygen levels, the state of her disrupted household were the rituals of our holiday season.

With the strength of a thousand horses, she willed herself to recovery within two weeks, without once going to the hospital, just video consultations with her doctor. She lectured her husband to drink more water, arranged for a caregiver for Carla, prepared meals all on her own, tended to their garden single-handedly, communicated with her children who were worried sick, signed her retirement papers, turned over her laptop and finally fed the cat! She was dauntless and steadfast as she always was. The coronavirus never stood a chance against her.

Her husband recovered, so did Carla. The caregiver returned and the cat was fed. As though it was another regular day, she announced her post-retirement preoccupation: learning desserts in preparation for Valentine's Day and perhaps learning to operate the electric sewing machine. On a Zoom Sunday with the family, when they were all breathing normally again, she proudly produced her blueberry strawberry tart for their threesome Valentine celebration. Always the consummate homemaker, she proudly displayed her talents at keeping an immaculate home, the lessons you taught her very early on.

Thank goodness for Fernando's strength. You, my second son, our fourth child, born on the anniversary day of the Fall of Bataan, when our soldiers fought alongside the Americans against the Japanese enemy during World War II. I thought you would be our last child. We named you Fernando after the vice-president of the Republic, who was our friend and client. He and his wife both stood as your godparents during your baptism, and how your mother and I beamed that our child should be christened in such illustrious company.

We built the summer home of the second most powerful man in the northern city where pine trees surrounded us every day. Your mother and I worked together as a successful team. She applied her marvellous architectural hand to draw the houses and I ensured the strength of these homes with the solid touch of an engineer. The vice-president was enamoured by our team-up—a romantic professionalism that was a novelty in the post-war era. You were born in an era of our conjugal prosperity.

You grew up with a quiet intensity, sometimes too deep for me to fathom. It's as if you and Ramon were two parts of myself—one gregarious and funny, the other serious and driven, eager to leave an imprint. You are steady and reliable. When I need fresh seafood, I call on you to take us out to the bay. I must remind you to call your lawyer and settle our accounts soon.

I admire his sturdiness as you do, Dad. I told him once of my abiding admiration and affection, and I think it might have embarrassed him.

He doesn't seem to know his own strength, his boldness. A stallion without fear, he charges on. Quietly, with grace and a firm grip. He is never loud, but is steadfast, as you know him, as he has always been.

You must have taught him that. You must have somehow inculcated in him the notion that he should be stronger than the rest of us; maybe preparing him for another role, another expectation. Those that cannot be apportioned to the oldest with his numerous responsibilities, nor to the youngest who must somehow be spared of a few burdens. He dispenses his family duties with diligence: organizes household budgets; prepares Mom's financial schedules so that she does not fret; attends to the repairs of her home where she now lives alone; informs all of us what he has accomplished. All in a day's work, and he remains cheerful. You have taught him so very well.

It is his outlook on life that you will be so proud of, Dad. He talks about gratitude for the blessings that have come his way. The good life that he has lived and continues to. The forgiveness for past hurts that he won't even remember. Nary an ounce of bitterness despite his own share of trials. He is a man at peace. And strength. And fortitude.

He talked lately about every day as an additional gift. Of course, I pray in my heart that he will have a long arc of life. To enjoy his children and grandchildren. To eat more of his favourite food because he loves to eat as we all do. To have earthly time with us.

We have been apart for a long time now because of this pandemic, and we wish so much to see each other. Your six children miss being with each other, despite our differences, our choices, our politics!

Teresita, my third child. Are you finally coming home? You've been gone so long. One time, long ago, we thought you would never awaken. The bad milk spoiled your stomach and you vomited for several days.

You were born at a time when prosperity dodged our lives. You were named after the patron saint of a thousand roses. But you were always frail, and your mother waited for your last breath.

We gave you the Extreme Unction. If you should die, then at least you would have been baptized a Catholic.

But you lived! Your mother would remind you each time you put your life in some danger. Like joining this activist organization, protesting in the streets. You were hardly studying, I know.

I came home, Dad. I broke down when I saw you suffering so much in your hospital room. I was so unprepared for what I saw. I had just spoken to you a week ago when you entered the hospital. It was a mild stomach bug, you said. You wanted to make sure you were well enough to enjoy the Christmas meal with your children when they arrived. You never left the hospital. When you did, you were a hollow body. On the phone when I said goodbye, you were a tiny breath. It was a very late night in Boston, and it was cold, and I was alone when you left me, when you left us. Your spirit had left while I was still clutching the phone, for you to stay on even for a little while.

But it felt like yesterday, or last week when you told my brother to call me in Boston, for me to return home. Urgently, as you requested. No, as you commanded. And I did not jump from the dining table at my landlord's home, because it was Christmas evening and I was all alone the entire holiday season. And dinner was good, the evening was warm of friendship and affection. My landlord played the piano and belted out celebratory songs. I postponed the call. I was afraid of what my brother would say.

I delivered the eulogy on behalf of my family. I spoke about their remembrances of you. Each one had a unique story. It affirmed how differently we experienced you as a father, how loving you were to us all.

I told that large gathering in the church how you were always proud of me, and how my heart would swell. And yet when I failed, you taught me to be gracious in defeat.

'We don't always win,' you said. 'But it is how we handle defeats that matter.'

To be sure, I have gone through life with several setbacks, some very large ones, but I always knew that I could rise again.

The defeats did come, Dad. A few more heartaches mostly. The last one drove me to live abroad again so I could heal and nourish my broken spirit. That January morning, when I opened the doors of my new home. There were two white butterflies that kissed me on the shoulder and then flew back into the cool morning air. Fast and fleeting. Gone before I made sense of that spiritual moment.

I was sure it was you. You visited me, approved this step I had taken to recover and rebuild what I felt was another shattered piece of me.

From there on, I was a different person. Pain re-shaped me. I carved out a piece for myself in this world. Since that butterfly moment, I flourished. Lived and travelled everywhere, met a wonderful man, remarried, gained a daughter, a son-in-law, a grandson and soon thereafter, another granddaughter. My in-laws multiply. I keep discovering them, scattered everywhere in the world. We love to meet each other as if all the years apart should be recovered quickly before time runs out.

Life is full, Dad. My cup runneth over.

And I was in a hospital too, Dad. Twenty-five days. It's called COVID. A nasty virus, worse than its predecessor. We are so afraid for Mom, so we shield her, and we keep away. We haven't seen her for over a year.

Every day in the hospital, I thought of you, my life, if there would be a future. I was so afraid of possibly not having one, of not ever leaving the hospital. Of dying alone. Bereft. It was terrifying.

I wondered if you would come into my dreams to fetch me, to take my hand and escort me to the life beyond this mortal world. I imagined you with a youthful tan, ruddy cheeks, lean, standing upright. A big wide smile that showed all your upper teeth. Dressed in your favourite jacket, the one you always wore during a journey.

But you never came, and I didn't see you. It wasn't time yet and my life as a mortal is not over.

My children, please tell your mother, that she is the gift of a lifetime. Tell her how radiant she was when I first saw her, a long time ago, in the Pavilion of the Manila Hotel. I could barely concentrate. I gathered all my courage and asked her to dance. Yes, what a lithe dancer she was, and I thought I should not feel complete until I saw her again.

How do I tell you, dearest Aida, that these fifty-three years have not been easy, I know, but that I have loved you in my imperfect way? That I am a flawed creature with an impetuous heart.

You, my wife, stood and stayed by me, when my health was strong, and when it faded away. How do I tell you how precious you are for waking up with me these past many years when I would nebulize so that my breath would last longer? I know you hardly slept, because I would wake up in the dark, soaked with sweat, and you would quietly tame your fear. I felt your helplessness as you painfully watched my health shrivel like a prune.

I have been so unable to care for you. I cannot even manage to walk any more. I could not comfort you when you felt ill. You worried so much for me. Then your nerves frayed with anxiety.

I need to comfort you now. To tell you that our life together was filled with many, very precious moments. I want you to keep those memories on your journey. Because I know, from the sound of my breath, that I cannot be with you much longer.

I called you early this morning. It was our fifty-fourth anniversary. One of the few times I remembered to call you. How many times did I forget to make that precious phone call? Was it because I thought we would always be around each other, together?

It does not feel that way any longer. Who knows if we will have another year again? I thanked you for the fifty-four years that you stayed as my wife. I asked you to come soon, quickly. To ask your forgiveness. To love you with my remaining breath. I need to look at you and to touch your face, to stroke your hair, to hold you again, and again, and again, before time runs out and I can no longer feel the nearness of your skin.

One day, perhaps in a dream when you visit me, Dad, could you tell me if I was a good daughter? If I ever hurt you in any way? And how could I have been a better daughter to you? So that you can wash away my regrets that remain. Not too many, but there are a few that linger.

It has been a long time since you last visited me in my dreams. Please visit me again.

Chapter 11

Tomb and Tower, Shrine and Synagogue

I visited the Jewish Museum in Berlin on a bright summer's day in August 2016. The grey hue of the museum's walls felt like an impenetrable fortress that deflected the sunlight. Its cold exterior projected architectural gloom, none of the majestic glass-and-metal structure of the Louvre Pyramid in Paris or the spiral ramp of the Guggenheim Museum in Bilbao that leads to a sunlit dome. The Jewish Museum is constructed as serial 'gashes', 'slits' and 'slashes' through which slivers of light pass. Even while Berliners named the museum 'the blitz', a YouTube commentator disagrees:

Not a thunderbolt, but a scar.

Walking down the narrow corridors lead to the Holocaust Tower, a twenty-four-metre-tall, dank and dark space with a single shaft of light coming through a small opening high up in the ceiling. My breath quickened; the narrowness was stifling. I gasped. In the distance are sounds streaming into the tower: children's voices, the noise of the streets, the clanging of church bells, life humming by. If one is denied the passing ice-cream truck and the music from the park, it is because one is a Jew.

The Polish-American architect, Daniel Libeskind, designed the Jewish Museum in Berlin as a 'dynamic zig-zag of buildings', meant to deliberately induce disorientation as one steps into its uneven lines and spaces. A narrator on YouTube describes the main building as an

> . . . abrupt zinc-clad extension that sits quietly disconnected and in contrast with its surroundings.

The entrance to the museum is the original baroque building that was seized by the Nazis in 1938. Marien Kruger, the museum's curator talks about the architect's motivation to destabilize visitors so as to mirror

> . . . even just a little bit the difficulty of German-Jewish history.

One does not come to the Jewish Museum to marvel. It won't qualify to the list of top-ten museums in Europe. According to Libeskind,

> It's not made for cinematographic or filmic reasons . . . but to connect to some form of experience that I think is important to communicate.

One comes here to remember and to honour the millions of murdered Jews. It is to them that this museum was dedicated. Remembrance however is a past littered with the presence of uneasy ghosts.

The Holocaust Tower is a living tomb. Jews were once brought here before they were deported to the gas chambers. They walked among the living, but their spirits were already dead. Their demise foretold; the silence of the foreboding walls signalled their coming desolation.

Adjacent to the tower is the Garden of Exile. I entered. Forty-nine concrete columns stand diagonally erect on a sloping patch of land. The columns were thick and sturdy. They leaned into me. I thought they would fall and crush me. The spaces between them were mere inches, evoking dizziness and a falling sensation. I felt as though I would fall into the abyss. At other times, a claustrophobic choking as the air between the columns is thin and sparse.

Barely five minutes in the garden and a sense of place is lost along with one's bearings. Standing on the grass on uneven terrain triggers a sense of panic, searching for balance and stability. I left very quickly to arrest the onset of vertigo. A sign at the entrance to the garden warned of physical disorientation.

This must be the emotional geography of forced separation and impending death. A bit like COVID when the virus lodged into my body and I knew instinctively that something had happened, something terribly frightening, an oracle of unforetold dangers. It reminded me of the emotions that enveloped me at the entrance to the Holocaust Tower.

Shortly after my Berlin visit, I flew to Israel. It was never an easy journey to this country: so upbeat and then so anxious; so threatened, and then so exuberant. As in the rituals of Purim and the candle celebrations at dusk during the Shabbath, and the visit to Rachel's Tomb to pay homage to women who labour at birth. Or entering the eight gates of Jerusalem. Magnificent but disturbing.

I walked with pilgrims towards the birthplace of Jesus on Nativity Square in Bethlehem, discovered an ancient church beneath the floorboards to reveal Byzantine art. The solemnity is thick, and the pilgrims are wrapped in sacredness. And the vibrant technological innovations in Tel Aviv, their jumpy bars and culinary experiments. The loud voices of bar guests watching the championship soccer match. Exhilarating.

But border crossings into Jerusalem are tense, and so is entering or leaving Israel via the King Hussein's Bridge entering Jordan. Israeli youths on mandatory military service patrol these crossings. They are sprightly, nimble, ready at the trigger. Someone's youthful impetuousness, another regular hothead, might just start another border conflagration.

This country is perpetually seething. Everywhere, everyday there is an undercurrent of something troubling. It is recent, it is ancient. It happens, of all places, on the city tram.

So many sentiments converge and collide on Jerusalem's Green Line. The passenger tram runs across the east and the west every day, in intervals of about fifteen minutes. In that waiting time, anything might happen. A stabbing, and then a scream. Or a sudden unexpected reunion with one's long-lost cousin from Ethiopia, and all the nasty memories of that exodus. Or Orthodox Jews hurrying towards Shabbat while Palestinians turn to face Mecca for early evening prayers. This tram bisects Jewish West and Arab East. It reflects all that is Israel.

It is never about just coexisting in this land with all of its claims to history and identity. Borders move, landscapes change. With them, relationships, attitudes, outlooks, emotions, actions. Someone will build a home, another's home will be demolished. Someone will settle, another will be imprisoned. There will be staunch resistance as there has always been since the birth of Israel. It must be the most intense human experience of all. Never has the beginning of a nation been so fraught with fear, fight and flight.

But there is also the Israel of kibbutzim where Tzip, my aunt-in-law lived. My husband, Yaakov, a Spanish-Moroccan Jew, visited her yearly. She was ninety-seven years old, the only remaining parent figure left in his life. As with all other Jews, Yaakov has lost so many of his loved ones. A few are left, they are scattered everywhere in the world. He doesn't speak much about them.

I nudged him: 'Find them before they disappear altogether.'

'Gathering them together,' he said, 'would be like holding grains of sand for a while; then they slip through the gaps in your fingers.

'I've wrapped those memories in a mental box,' he continued, 'and buried them deep underneath. Some events shouldn't be remembered.'

But he spoke to his aunt Tzip often; swapped stories on the phone with Era, Hagi, Tim, his far-flung cousins. Lunched happily some years ago with another long-lost, but recently discovered, cousin in Berlin. They seem to gradually re-emerge out of the Jewish woodwork, slowly peering to check the world that could at times be safe.

It is mostly during the winter when we visited our aunt Tzip. I clung to her as she clings to her fragile life. Her Nepalese caregiver wrapped a blanket across her skinny frame, and she disappeared into the folds of big woollen stitches. Our visits always reminded me of my religious roots in Judaism and the troubled history of these two religions. But more, I regretted the years that I didn't know her, and how I wished I did.

With my shrunken Jewish family, we spent an afternoon in a Palestinian restaurant close to Bethlehem near the abominable wall. Christian icons peered down on us while we feasted on seared meats and pickled side dishes. The smell of roasted coffee beans massaged our nostrils. A whiff of rosewater wafted across the restaurant. I was sated with sumptuous Palestinian food, in awe of how so much suffering can still produce gratifying meals. Outside, cars were parked directly on the wall. Graffiti screamed, protested: this divide must end.

On a separate visit, cousin Era drove us to the Dafna kibbutz in southern Israel on a Friday afternoon in 2016. Several residents gathered for an evening celebration. A female rabbi with a massive crop of dark curly locks was dressed in a fashionable, white, lace blouse and slender slacks. She was a pristine picture of the subtle reinterpretation of the traditional male-led, Jewish, weekly ritual of the Shabbat.

There was much singing in this communal hall of the kibbutz where, on Friday evenings, the common space turned into a modernized version of a synagogue. There was a small band—a pianist, a percussionist and a guitarist—all of them accompanied the worshippers who launched into fervent singing. When the music tempo increased, the female drummer struck her drum with more ferocity and the male guitarist strummed the six nylon strings with more force. The attendees broke out into dance. Their voices, pitched louder, the decibels, higher, their vocal cords strained to prolong the notes. Their young children also joined in the revelry of their parents and their grandparents. They testified to the intergenerational commitment to faith and to the enduring practice of kibbutz communalism despite Israel's own shift towards harder-edged capitalism.

Several generations of Israelis no longer live in the kibbutzim. They have taken up urban lifestyles in Jerusalem and Tel Aviv, and regard kibbutz homes as a kind of weekend country retreat if their parents and grandparents still live there.

This larger context of Israel's spiritual practices is of course dominated by Israel's legendary conflict over the Temple Mount, also known as the Al Aqsa Mosque. Both the Jews and the Muslims claim ownership over this sacred place, both revere it within their religious traditions. Blood has been spilled and tears, shed over this piece of contested territory, all 6 square kilometres of it. It is a site of so much grief, as though the long-drawn-out centuries of misunderstanding are contained within this tiny, embittered space.

But on the Friday evening of the Shabbat at Dafna kibbutz, there is none of that rancour. There are only Jews in prayer. I must be the lone, curious, Christian interloper. It is an hour devoted to public worship for private purposes, as one twenty-six-year-old told me.

'I'm not religious,' Nof said, 'but this gives me a connection to something private that I feel inside, something I cannot talk about easily. The singing helps me feel these private emotions.'

Her mother Era told me that the loss of her son, Yaar, during the war with Lebanon in 2006 was a tragedy for the family. He was barely eighteen years old when he was killed on the last day of the war. When the war ended, the boy, whom they expected to return to Nahsholim Kibbutz, was a corpse. Four years later, Era's husband and Nof's father, died of illness. It was too much for Nof who was barely in her twenties to fathom all this death. She interrupted her studies, left for Australia, and heavily tattooed her arms.

'To invite the pain and control it,' her mother says. 'It is how she deals with her losses.'

Nof left again for Dharamsala in northern India, hoping to meet her aunt who has travelled there for over a decade. Their wandering spirits are a salve to their losses. Or perhaps an ancient Biblical sentiment where Jews wander the earth in search of their inner peace, their Promised Land.

'To inhale the pure air of the Himalayas,' she said. 'It is clean, no scent of death. Just the quiet mountains where I don't have to feel anything.'

The Friday evening of the Shabbat celebration was purposeful. Everyone was dressed in white—a colour to dispel the darkness and heal the hearts blackened by sorrow. Everyone must have lost someone, whether to a war or a genocide and maybe even just death by natural causes. But there's been too much dying already; much of it perhaps senseless, like Yaar's death, one day before the war ended.

They come together every week to renew and celebrate their faith, if not in an Eternal Being, at least to life that they still retain. The Lord is somewhere here amongst them in this makeshift synagogue. He is in the nylon strings of the guitarist, between the fingers of the lady drummer, in everyone's vocal cords. Every note that is hummed and played brings the Spirit back, perhaps because it is the one thing that protects them from believing that life is nothing but a betrayal.

The two candles are lit on the Shabbat altar, many more burn on a side table around which the residents gather in a last moment of fellowship. The candlelight flickers on, well into the sunset.

***

I pondered on Era's shrine to her son, Yaar, in her home at Naksholin Kibbutz against everything that I saw at the Jewish Museum just days before. Her fresh, white walls, was where sunlight poured in unremittingly. Sounds of neighbours sat around in their patios, chatting. There was a life-sized photograph of her son, Yaar, in the centre of the kitchen wall. Strips of bright red, handwoven fabric from Uzbekistan adorned the sides of the photograph. Fresh flowers added more colour.

Her grief, more than a decade later, is bathed in colourful artwork. On the wall, her son lives on. He gazes down at her while she sips her morning coffee, watches her move from kitchen to terrace. She inspects the grass on her lawn, wondering how fast they will grow this winter. He wants to tell her to be patient. Grass will grow at its own pace. And then she is reminded how young boys, trained to fight wars so early on, are full of their own wisdom.

***

Tzip, Era's mother and my aunt-in-law, passed away in the same house that had she lived in for seventy-eight years, in Neot Mordechai kibbutz, in the northern Galilee region in Israel. Her daughters Era and Yagi sat in *shiva*, the Jewish ritual of mourning. Her final goodbye on the phone was with her son Yuval in San Diego. Like him, we missed her funeral ceremony. The pandemic grounded us.

Always the pandemic. This virus has kept us away from all of those we wish to be close to. Whether in life or in death.

'I feel tired,' she said to us on the phone a few months before she passed. She could barely speak, the struggle of conveying her feelings travelled through the cable wires. We knew she was saying goodbye in advance, just so she didn't miss out anyone to whom she wanted to bid farewell.

'*Ani ohev otakh*,' she said to me in Hebrew on my first visit in 2014, my first ever sight of her. We sat in her garden and there was a single hibiscus in bloom as she spoke.

I took Hebrew lessons so I could speak to her. To tell her that I loved her back, like a daughter loves her mother . . . so much, but never sufficiently. But we lost time and I couldn't say goodbye.

We scoured the Israeli websites for florists. I chose the white lilies, pure as I have always known her. Old and untainted. She had shed the cares of the world; she spent her last years, purifying and emptying herself. She left me with that lesson. She is buried in the same plot of land where her grandson was laid to rest in 2006.

Nof wrote a eulogy from India to her grandmother. She traced her grandmother's history, her arrival in Israel in 1939 after a harrowing escape from the Nazis. Tzip was a young teenager at the time when she left the Austrian city of Gretz which was, by then, overrun by the Nazis.

She witnessed the horrific murder of her mother by the Nazis. She and her sister prepared for the voyage to Israel to undertake *aliyah*—the migration to Israel. They both sailed on a small ship together with 1,200 Jewish youths. They arrived in Czechoslovakia where they waited for larger ships to take them to Israel.

But World War II broke out and the borders were closed. The Jewish youths were stranded in in Yugoslavia. The Nazis slaughtered most of them. Only 200 teenagers survived. Tzip was one of them.

Continuing the trip to Turkey and Lebanon after the war, Tzip finally arrived in Israel at the Atlit illegal immigration camp. From there she entered school and studied Hebrew, agriculture and home economics.

She met Dov, a soldier in the Israeli army, whom she married. In 1949, they moved to Kibbutz Neot Mordechai where Tzip worked in a children's home, a clothing store, a feeding kitchen for children and a shoe factory called Teva Naot. The Yaar shoe model was one of the factory's productions. It was also the name of her grandson who was killed in the Lebanon War of 2006. Nof recalled the shoes of her choice, the Forest model, which her grandmother made.

Life in the kibbutz finally settled for Tzip. She outlived her husband. Her mortal remains are still in the kibbutz where her life as an Israeli began and ended.

The peripatetic grandchild Nof, heard about her death in India. She eulogized her grandmother through a poem. We received a copy via email. As in all facets of life during the pandemic, we grieved and felt our losses digitally.

Despite all the grief, loss and difficulty,
Tzip lived proudly

Hardworking, dedicated, a strong,
Determined, independent woman

Pleasant-mannered and
Exceptionally sharp-witted

With a clear mind in a warm bed,
Full head of hair,
Eyes that see everything,
And a ninety-seven-year memory

The soul that was Tzip
The soul that taught me to live
The beloved and only grandmother
I have known all my life
In its precise Austrian time,
In good return and love all around
Continued tonight to the next world

This is the story of her soul,
Her fascinating journey
In this body, in this incarnation, in this time

Who will give and
Your soul will continue peacefully home
Until next time we meet

Thank you for giving me life
Thank you for teaching me to stay in it

Despite the difficulty
The pain and the loss
You taught me
A strong heart on shaky ground

I'm standing here today
Descendant
Of a strong and powerful female lineage

With pain in all my bones
On your shoulder

Remember your journey
And I will not forget
Until my last day.

I continued my Hebrew lessons, nonetheless, perhaps for when Tzip and I meet in Heaven. So I can say *toda raba* (thank you so much), for holding my hand, for speaking my Catholic name, for asking me to stay longer at our very first meeting, almost as though she had waited for me all her life.

Perhaps these undercurrents will be muted for a short while and the seething will soften. When I find comfort in Tzip's death, when I can visit Israel once again, though a bit emptier this time. When the sorrow passes through me like morning mist and her death will calm my unease.

As it did when I arrived on the third floor of the Jewish Museum in Berlin through the longest pathway, which Libeskind called the Axis of Continuity—the continuity of Jewish presence in Germany and the world over. It was a set of big, bright rooms, sectioned off by small showcases of Jewish daily life in the earliest years in Germany when Jews lived there without incident. There were drawings of children's art, model designs of synagogues, photographs of the everyday, Shabbat celebrations laid out on wooden tables, goblets, plates, bread, with music wafting across the rooms.

Suddenly, at the turn of a corner, there are bare black blocks. Nothing hangs on them. Only darkness. It envelops the corridors. You pass through them and there is a very quiet danger. Libeskind called these spaces 'voids'.

Past these foreboding walls was a pomegranate tree, its fruit of the brightest red, the symbol of Jewish life. There it stood regally, at the centre of the large room. An iron staircase led to the very top of the tree, and one could post a secret wish to hang on its branches. I posted my own: I wish to see Tzip again.

But I won't, I can't. This pandemic is a long discontinuous moment that keeps us away from those we love. This virus created these darkened voids of separation.

But I believe in hope, the most continuous human sentiment there is. That was when I remembered the pomegranate tree in Era's garden. There is continuity in life despite this pandemic.

I hope to linger at Tzip's grave in Neot Mordechai, with each carefully placed stone, a beautiful memory of her brief life with me. Fold my hands in prayer, whisper to the heavens hoping that my message would reach her: *toda rabah*. Thank you so much, because I met you and knew you. Fleetingly, yes. But it felt like you were always there.

Thus, will I end the void of separation.

Chapter 12

Sex and the Virus in the City

Consider this fifty-five-year old woman. At the height of the Singapore lockdown called the 'circuit breaker' in April 2020, she ran an advertisement in the classified ads section of an un-nameable website to offer massage services. Colloquially, she meant 'I give you happy ending.' Presumably, to alleviate your suffering from a most unhappy lockdown.

A sixty-seven-year-old male, best left unnamed (you can Google this story if your wish), responded to the ad. He booked her services that included massage, masturbation and pubic hair trimming for two hours, all at the cost of approximately US$120. That would translate to approximately US$1 per minute.

Depending on how you want to look at this transaction, the cost was not worth the risk of being discovered by the authorities, fined and possibly jailed for flouting the lockdown. Or you could consider this as a rare economic opportunity that does not come (pun unintended) too often when the entire country is cocooned at home, waiting for the moment of epiphany. Calculating humans that we are, they figured: give and take pleasure; reduce pain; end the isolation, albeit temporarily; make a little money. Everybody wins.

Which our intrepid entrepreneur did. Customer and provider both had a happy ending. And then shortly thereafter, a not-so-happy one.

They were both caught when a nearby resident reported to the police that the massage shop was reportedly open because of human movement in and out of the shop and a humming air-conditioner. The short-lived pleasure was followed by long virtual trips to the courthouse.

She was charged for operating a business without a licence, disobeying the lockdown restrictions even after having been notified that she does not operate an 'essential' service, and therefore endangered the public. Mr Happy Ending Customer received a conditional twelve-month warning for breaching safe-distancing measures. Whereas Ms Masseuse was slapped with a fine of approximately US$17,000, all of which she settled after pleading guilty to the court and avoided jail term. As per media coverage, court deliberations were prolonged due to Ms Masseuse's massive crying and pleading. She further argued her case: she massaged his kidney for health purposes, a skill she learned in China. She obliged the customer's request '. . . then the customer asked for the frontal part.'

I read this story during my long stay at the hospital. I called it 'confinement amusement' to forget the discomfort of nasal swabs. When it came to sex, I figured, human ingenuity knew no bounds. No virus could kill the sexual imagination, no pandemic could bridle the urge. Diminished, maybe. Reduced frequency, for sure. But totally eliminated? Never. Chasing pleasure of the sexual kind was as essential as drawing breath.

History bears testimony to this sine qua non. Neanderthals, apparently, did kiss. Not just grunt, grind, gobble and bump, so claims Zaria Gorvett in a BBC publication dated January 2021. This definitive piece of evidence came from the dental plaque of Neanderthal's teeth found in northern Spain and from the Denisovans, cave dwellers in Russia's Altai mountains. DNA samples revealed that there was interbreeding between the two species through the discovery of a bone fragment belonging to a girl nicknamed Denny. Her father was a Denisovan and her mother was a Neanderthal. The transfer of oral microbes between Neanderthals and Denisovans through DNA sampling was documented as far back as 120,000 years ago. The samples suggested that lips did lock, and bodies did mate, otherwise how was Denny produced?

The harbinger of sexual mores, the seventeenth-century Puritans offered other surprises. Professor Lisa Wade at Tulane University argued that sex in the Puritan era was a feature of settler colonialism:

> Colonizing the US was a dangerous job; lots of people were dying from exposure, starvation, illness, and war. Babies replenished the labor supply, motivating the Puritans to channel the sex drive towards the one sexual activity that made babies: intercourse.

A deviant Puritan who transgressed these norms could be fined, whipped and ostracized through the infamous 'scarlet letter'. Argument settled. We've come to believe this version of transgressions against accepted conduct of human sexuality as conventional wisdom ever since.

Always having had a bad rap for hyper-conservative morality, deemed impractical and unrealistic, Puritan sexuality was debunked by Madeline Bilis of the *Boston* magazine debunked this myth. Bilis wrote about Anne Bradstreet who was a poet and who waxed lyrical about Puritan sexual desires in 1630, hers in particular. In the context of that era, the poem was considered erotic literature, possibly equivalent to Pauline Réage's *Story of O* or Henry Miller's *Tropic of Cancer*. The poem never saw print.

> Whom whilst I 'joy'd, nor storms, nor frosts I felt,
> His warmth such frigid colds did cause to melt.

The two historians, Sarah Handley-Cousins and Marissa Rhodes, went further in debunking the myths of Puritan sexuality. First, there was an enormous backlog of cases on sexual deviance according to William Bradford, governor of Plymouth, who admitted to

> . . . breaking out of sundry notorious sins.

The latter included pre-marital sex, extramarital sex and pregnancy out of wedlock.

Then there was 'junketing'—a seventeenth-century version of the 'petting parties' of the 1920s. Young men and women got together to laugh, dance, swap dirty jokes and engage in debauchery. Junketing was hypersexual dancing, the historians reported, and the colonial authorities were not pleased even while some of them blinked. Says Mather, a member of a noted Puritan clan of preachers,

> . . . the very motion of the body which is used in dancing has a palpable tendency to that which is evil . . .

Yet junketing continued.

And then 'bundling'—the Puritan version of dating-cum-sleep-over with parental 'consent'. Young people who went a-courting often into the wee hours of the night would simply sleep over, with the parents in the next room who could oversee the goings-on late at night, presumably even in their sleep. Mostly, the domestic rules came down to remaining fully clothed waist down. But in the off chance that the daughter did get pregnant, given human weaknesses at nocturnal patrolling, the perpetrator was easily identifiable, avoiding community scandal and speculation. The widespread practice was rather popular that it caused an unnamed songwriter to eulogize it, albeit humorously.

> *A bundling couple went to bed*
> *With all their clothes from foot to head*
> *That the defense might seem complete*
> *Each one was wrapped in a sheet*
> *But O! this bundling's such a witch*
> *The man of her did catch the itch*
> *And so provoked was the wretch*
> *That she of him a bastard catch'd*

While the Puritans were not the sexiest religious reformers, Bilis concluded, they were not an altogether repressed bunch either, as later generations were made to believe. Rather, there were nuanced ways of circumventing and re-interpreting everyday practice, despite laws and strictures that enforced conformity of sexual behaviour. The Puritan story is a gleeful reminder that their legacy to human sexuality is far more complex than we have been led to believe.

While Puritan history disabused us of the notion of human prudery writ large, it was in the decade of the 1960s when rampaging hormones went into full display. The debunking of conservative sexual mores was the most blatant and comprehensive. It began with Betty Friedan's famous dictum: 'the problem with no name' as the defining sentiment in the age of dissatisfaction. The burning of the bra, the explosion in contraceptive use among women and the hippie culture of the 1960s, all converged in a decade marked by challenges to entrenched cultural norms and practices.

In music, the Beatles and the Rolling Stones epitomized the shifting and shaking of tectonic plates in human sexuality. Mick Jagger's 'Let's Spend the Night Together' and 'I Can't Get No Satisfaction' were matched by the Beatles' 'A Hard Days' Night', such songs were suggestive of sexuality coming out of the closet. Other groups followed suit very quickly, their songs brought to the very edge of what began as a flirtation with homosexuality. The Kinks from the United Kingdom released 'Dedicated Follower of Fashion'. The Who, another British musical group, released 'I'm a Boy' in 1966 and topped at number two in the musical charts. It was a song that detailed the angst of a boy whose mother wanted him to be a girl. It may have been prescient of the gender identity discourse that would arrive full force in the post-modern world in the twenty-first century.

Then there's the evolution of our mating language. During the flower-power era which designated the 1960s and the 1970s counter revolution, talk was all about 'freaks getting high and sharing sex.' The terms really meant LSD-induced orgies. Except that no one ever bothered to include the harsh reality of tissue-and-towel supply for post-orgy, coital clean-up once the hallucinations ended. Logistics matter even during sexual revolutions.

The cult movie *Bob and Carol and Ted and Alice* added to the spice of sexualized language: 'spouse-swapping', 'open marriage' and 'swinging couples'. In the movie, two suburban couples emerged from a weekend retreat at Esalen Institute in Southern California, all gung-ho to experiment on complete honesty that included confessing to sexually desiring your best-friend's spouse. Actually, writes movie critic Roger Ebert, the movie was

> . . . not about wife-swapping at all, but about the epidemic of moral earnestness that's sweeping our society right now . . .

a 1960s version of political correctness. The urge among couples to speak the truth in all its elaboration was what framed the open marriage ethos. Its awkward motto could very well have been: 'Screw your best-friend's spouse but always speak the truth.' I'm paraphrasing. The point being that, marriage, even of the open variety, was never served by the unvarnished truth about your hang-ups, only by a compact of trust and respect between both partners never to hurt and harm the relationship. And this would include, presumably, discretion about your deepest feelings and fantasies particularly if these concern your next-door neighbour and/or your best-friend's wife who may have a fetish about strutting around the yard or the garage in her underwear. Keep your fantasies to yourself; everyone deserves privacy.

The highest point of the revolution in sexual mores was Plato's Retreat in New York City, regarded as the 'most infamous sex club of the 1970s'. The owner, Larry Levenson, must have hit upon a unique insight about sex: the urge at exhibitionism and voyeurism. One went to Plato's Retreat to engage in heterosexual public mating; others went to watch public coupling. Both fetishes were a damn good business proposition.

Until the fear of a crashing immune system gripped the world in the 1980s and the revolution fizzled out. The other nasty virus, HIV, stifled the urge for promiscuity. Plato's Retreat closed its doors to the public in 1985. With tax evasion cases and an immunity-busting virus, Levenson's experiment screeched to a halt.

Traditionalists heaved a sigh of relief. Heterosexual monogamy staged a militant comeback.

Wrong, sorry. 'Safe sex' replaced sex-sharing. The term came into wide use for its singular, uncontested meaning: If you must indulge, please wear condoms. Human predilection for innovation prevailed.

Enter the age of the rubber revolution. This little contraption became the object of countless iterations at obtaining the best fit with the best feel. Bill without a surname, CEO of RipnRoll Inc., breaks down the history of the competition for the perfect condom. It began with the Japanese invention of the thinnest sheath to give both partners a feel for 'skinless skin' with unforgettable brands such as Beyond Seven, Crown Condoms and Kimono Microthin. Not to be outdone, the other condom manufacturers Carter Wallace and Ansell rolled out their Xtra Pleasure, Trojan Ultra Pleasure and Lifestyles Extra Pleasure with the friction-enhancer features. Later versions included multi-coloured, multi-flavoured condoms; others had spermicide as contraceptive bonus, and delaying lubricants for staying power and mutual stimulation. This application of human ingenuity, lest we forget, was the threat of HIV/AIDs. As the years and decades wore on without a definitive cure for HIV/AIDs, the condom became its best available protector against transmission of the virus. Abstinence would have been the best and only solution, but the most unrealistic one.

Then 'mechai' came along—the local term for condom in Thailand. Its rather illustrious history is in no way connected to the sexual revolution in the West, but a sexual revolution in Thailand nonetheless. Bear with me. The story is worth retelling.

In the 1970s, family planning and reproductive health came to Thailand in a rather curious way: via local vegetable farming in an urban space of 400 square metres. Customers who bought the vegetables received lace underwear as a bonus gift. The garden also housed the offices of the non-profit Population and Community Development Foundation. Its founder was Mechai Viravaidya.

In the 1990s when HIV/AIDs became Thailand's scourge, Mechai ventured into the restaurant business. He opened Cabbages and Condoms on the same plot of his vegetable garden. He began a campaign on HIV education in Thailand. With a stroke of genius, he combined sex education with Thai cuisine. One will never know how the revelation about human desire came to him—that somehow good food and safe sex were inextricably interlinked. It was a winning strategy. Cabbages and Condoms in Bangkok outlived and outshone all the innovations around brands and features of the fast-evolving condom. A quirky restaurant was irresistible.

Enter the restaurant in Bangkok's Soi 12 off of Sukhumvit, the city's main thoroughfare. A long entrance with thick foliage invites you inside. Ceiling lights wrapped in rubber illuminates the pathway to the main restaurant. The hanging lanterns are shaped as long prophylactics, drawing much laughter from customers.

It is not a cramped urban space, rather a sprawling edifice of zoned areas, a non-smoking section tucked away deeper into the garden. The stores right by the entrance sell paraphernalia: keychains, T-shirts, mugs, spoons, oral contraceptives and condoms of all shapes, colours, sizes and flavours. To facilitate the purchase, there are designations: politician size; coup d'état size; democracy size; military size. A witty poster pasted on the window reads: 'Sorry, we have no elections. Take a condom instead.'

By the entrance are life-sized mannequins, all their outfits fashioned out of condoms. A male's jersey has the number seventeen emblazoned in white rubber. Strips of contraceptive pills form the woman's belt buckle. The little girl's braids are hanging black condoms, her socks are white rubbers. Then there is the prized mannequin: Santa Claus with a full beard of white stretchable condoms, all for the pleasure of pulling and snapping them back into Santa's face.

Mechai's endeavours were not pure gimmickry. The results of his campaign were rather astounding. Fertility rates declined from a high of 6.42 children per woman in the 1960s to 2.60 in the 1980s, a 59.5 per cent decline. Over a period of twenty-five years, Thailand's fertility rate dropped by 60 per cent. HIV infection rates abated as well for the period 1985–2015. Julius Eleazar and eight other authors published a peer-reviewed article that categorically confirmed the change in sexual behaviour among the sexually active population due to the 100 per cent condom-use programme. While Mechai did not single-handedly change the course of HIV in Thailand, his efforts nonetheless were part of the larger public campaign against HIV.

From a culinary perspective, Cabbages and Condoms does not disappoint. Customers continue to flock to the restaurant for its crunchy papaya salad known as *somtam*, enveloped in honey-flavoured fish and peanut sauce. The fresh mango and coconut-doused sticky rice for desert clears up the palate after a heavy dose of chillies and lemongrass. Customers receive complimentary condoms attached to their bill. None of those boring after-dinner mints.

Wisecracking aside, there is homage to be paid. Today, Cabbages and Condoms proliferate. There is a branch in Chiang Rai in the north and Pattaya in the south. An overseas branch opened in Oxfordshire in the UK in 2012 and a franchise in Kumamoto prefecture in Japan. Mechai is synonymous to sound business practices in combination with social advocacies.

Bill and Melinda Gates awarded US$1 million to Mechai in 2007 in recognition of his pioneering work to family planning and HIV/AIDs prevention. His foundation, the Population and Community Development Association, is the largest NGO in Thailand, employing 600 staff and overseeing 120,000 volunteers. Not bad for someone who started out as a vegetable gardener. And his name is already immortalized.

Setting aside all social-marketing campaigns, the most reliable is still the 'blood test'. Its mere utterance conveys cold reality. Just facts. Medically certified. Evidence-based. No doubts, no spam, no slang, no spin. Final and finished.

A friend of mine once related to me her regular meet-up with a potential sex partner. Their frequent meetings had gone beyond cosy dinners and after-dinner drinks. It was time to escalate to the next stage of dating: sex. But first things first. He proposed, nay insisted, that they exchange blood-test results when they next met up at Starbucks. He included in his proposal the standard STD panel: HIV/AIDs, syphilis, chlamydia, gonorrhoea, herpes 1 and herpes 2.

I dared not ask if her carnal urges had just been quashed by this rather unsexy prologue. A medical certificate as foreplay? Who does that? Instead, I asked if the blood tests were worth it. Sheepish smile, then a giggle. I got my answer.

At the end of our meeting, she interjected. 'I asked him to include a sperm count.'

I splattered tea all over my blouse. I figured, she got slapped with such dowdy stipulations, so she upped the ante.

Enter the Virus. When COVID-19 struck, the libido's unbounded imagination during enforced isolation produced astonishing inventions, all of them online. The electronic age engulfed all our habits, including the ones in the bedroom.

Flashback to pre-2020. In the new millennium, sex went digital. It started with dating platforms. Nobody would dare admit then that they had surfed Match.com or Craigslist. It was an exclusive society of online-dating partners, all sworn to secrecy that they met through a dating website.

Until the market exploded into finer segments of partner specs: a dating site for Christians, Catholics, single, newly singled, married but playing around, casual, serious, short-term, threesome, twosome, hetero, homo and various other kinky unmentionables. The varieties are endless: from same-faith to same-sex liaisons, the digital marketplace took over the traditional functions of peer-to-peer networking. No need for your friend to introduce you to their best friend. Matchmakers had to scale up their services that ranged from due diligence for potential mates (a form of spying really) to astrological charts plucked from the Internet. One might call it algorithm-induced coupling.

The mating calls went digital. When checking Google for the ten best dating sites, Tinder and BumbleBee occupy top position, the first one for easy and fast hook-ups, the second for confident women. Coffee Meets Bagels refer to curated matches called 'bagels' every day at noon, and Plenty of Fish is, well, fishy, according to one reviewer, because it's lots of bots and scams rather than potential partners. The League is an elite dating app which asks for your job, college and LinkedIn profile. There are also geography-specific dating apps: Quora in India; Peekawoo in the Philippines; Amanda in South Korea; It's Just Lunch in Singapore. The finer distinctions between these providers could end up as fodder for a book of literary essays, a memoir, a conference paper, or a doctoral dissertation.

The virus threatened to spoil the party. For starters, lockdown-induced stress dissipated hormonal rages. If you're cohabitating, too much togetherness dampened the libido. Divorce rates have gone up during the pandemic. Couples discovered how truly incompatible they were. Screeching kids and the pressures of homework added to the burden of a suddenly intense homelife. No sleepovers, no pyjama parties, no summer camp. Exhausted by hyper-domesticity, who had time to even get horny?

Or for others, there were moments of rediscovery. Suddenly touching each other's hands at the kitchen while slathering mayonnaise on an egg salad became a prelude to intimacy. Postponed dates of the past became fulfilled promises under quarantine. There's time to Netflix together while eating brownies in bed at midnight. There's no pressure to rise at 8 a.m. for a morning conference. Besides, the pool and gym are closed.

Or couples on long-distance mode endured the new rituals of travel: seventy-two-hour PCR tests; two-week quarantine on arrival and return; permissions and travel clearances from their respective authorities. A close friend, separated from his wife for eighteen months, endured the month-long preparations to get her home after she received her vaccine. Tickets booked and rebooked, airport transfers arranged, accredited hotel rooms reserved. The final swab test is six days away. He waits dutifully some four blocks from where she is lodged, makes sure that she is as close to him as possible. Their one joy: they waved frantically at each other while her shuttle bus passed the entrance of his condo, the first time in over a year that they both see each other in the flesh—masked, gloved, face-shielded, physically distanced. It will be another excruciatingly long, seven-day wait until she enters the door to their home.

For singles, one-night stands continue unabated, according to a *Washington Post* article in August 2020. You'd think the practice would have been discarded just to avoid the obvious physical, not to mention, emotional risks. Nope. The virus failed to dampen the most primal of human urges, even though it may have caused a rejiggering of the most ancient of all human rituals: mating.

During the pandemic, hundreds of dating sites proliferated. They were the perfect antidote to lockdown boredom, unsatisfied carnality, emotional isolation and loneliness. Zoom never had it so good. A free subscription gives you free connection time for forty-five minutes. That's plenty when it comes to sizing up the outcomes of your app cruising. Best yet, cruisers are in full control. Zoom automatically disconnects after exhausting the quota. The leave button is but one click away should lack of interest override curiosity.

On both screens, there's just the two of you, ready for the exploration. Without having once stepped out of your house, paid for a drink at the bar, slapped on facial make-up and false eyelashes. You could, if you wanted to be really blasé about it, show up in your bottom pyjamas and top it with a sequined blouse or tight-fitting T-shirt that outline your sculpted abs. Neither is interested in what's below the waist. That's reserved for post-digital, physically distanced dating.

The back-and-forth interrogation is fairly straightforward. So much unlike the pick-up bars of the 1970s, no need for flirty eye contact or expensive cocktails; no witty, pick-up lines. It's all about digital efficiency. Casual sex in the age of corona is a clinical exercise, rather tedious, banal even, but mandatory.

'Have you quarantined?'

'When does yours end?'

'Have you been swabbed?'

'Did you get your PCR results yet?'

'Are you vaccinated?'

'First jab? Second jab? Boostered?'

Even during COVID recovery, the subject of sex is never far off. Check out any of the hundreds of Facebook support groups for long COVID and there's bound to be several entries on post-COVID sex. Whatever havoc the virus has wreaked on humanity, one of its upsides is the positive effect on one's sexual hormones. I kid you not: some reported feeling 'more randy' and 'scratchy' while waiting out the ending of long COVID. Here's a sample of online confessions:

'Not trying to be funny—has anyone experienced a higher sex drive? Or intense orgasms?'

'Oh my gosh yea it's like get a boost of damn sex energy and then when u do, ur shit starts to race and yea . . .'

'Honestly, I may have seen a higher sex drive, yes.'

'I wondered the same thing, especially since my main symptoms were heart-related, I didn't want to end up dying of a heart attack, lol. But I took the chance, after having to give up almost all other physical activities, I said I wouldn't give up sex even if it killed me. So far so good (although admittedly it's not as often as pre-COVID).'

It goes both ways: lockdown exacerbated domesticity and produced none-too-desirable results. COVID long haulers had more sexual energy and couldn't quite understand the uptake in sexual urges. Some couples rediscovered intimacy, even contributing to a baby boom. Lack of human contact enhanced the desire for human touch, sometimes lots of it, more than there ever was pre-pandemic.

The best part of it all? It's been two years of COVID. Humans have accepted that the virus will be around for a while. Similarly, humans haven't stopped, and won't stop thinking, talking and having sex. We won't let any virus do that.

Chapter 13

COVID United: A Family Pandemic Year

Shortly after my release from the hospital, Zoom became the platform for a weekly sibling discussion. The topic veered instantly to the subject of my mother's situation in Manila. Given her advanced age, we recognized that her health is in a very precarious state. As mentioned earlier, the rest of us were scattered in different parts of the globe except for two brothers who reside in Manila. What we needed, we all agreed, was a unified approach towards our mother who lived by herself along with her caregivers should she be infected with COVID.

The discussion went into overdrive for several weeks. Refinements and adjustments to the protocol were the staples of our weekly discussions. From ambulance calls to hospital admissions, the various steps were laid out in minute-by-minute detail that could rival any educator's lesson plan. Back-and-forth and side-to-side, we belaboured the very many possible questions for which there were fewer answers.

Truthfully, it wasn't fun at all. The discussions were a mixture of trying-hard-to-suppress emotions and hyper-detailed logistical planning. The tedium was matched by the grim possibility that, should she be infected, we may never see her at all. We have heard and read enough stories of infected patients who were moved from hospital wards to the crematorium, with nary a moment for vigils and burial rituals. We could very well have been planning her death without some of us. The thought crossed our minds many times: we have been saying goodbye to her with every phone call.

That was two years ago. Thankfully, the protocol remained an excruciating exercise in consensus-building among siblings who did not always agree with one another. Or, to be humorous about it, an opportunity for verbal fencing, sparring and repartee.

The one-page document remains filed in our six-sibling archive. I regard it as the site on which our energies which previously remained dormant as our separate lives across the globe barely intersected, were mobilized and consolidated by the reality that a rampaging virus could reach my mother's doorstep.

Two years later, my mother remains the proud inhabitant of an elaborate, six-bedroom house in the suburbs of Manila where she is comfortably ensconced, surrounded by open gardens that give her much room for morning breathing exercises and a daily walk to inspect the blooming bougainvillea trees arched into a fuchsia canopy. The cool blue waters of the swimming pool calm her amid her loneliness. No doubt, her house is an elegant venue for solitary life and lockdowns.

The sibling Zoom sessions moved into the discussion of forthcoming trips to Manila for the much needed and over-delayed visit. All of us, including my mother, have been vaccinated. The protocol changed to quarantine upon arrival and physical spacing inside my mother's home. This time, we planned for her ninety-ninth birthday celebration during the pandemic. This was worth every ounce of our time.

As a sociologist, observing family dynamics is always an exercise in abstraction about the larger dynamics of society. Sociology provides a discipline for family analysis and a theoretical coherence to what might seem interminable gaggle among its oftentimes rambunctious members. Emile Durkheim, the esteemed French sociologist, whose writings are considered sociological canon, considered the family as perhaps the most important of all social institutions. Family is the foundation of society and is at the core of what he calls 'mechanical solidarity'—the cohesion within family units that derives from bonds of kinship. A coalition of families forms clans, tribes, lineages, networks. Multiples segments branch outward. Through ritual kinship, larger networks proliferate. Hierarchies form. Then a society evolves, and with it, the principles and practices, the norms and values, the roles among family members that would regulate relationships between and among them. Society is a mosaic of family networks—the boundaries often stretched sideways to accommodate those whom we embrace as blood members and also as ritual kin.

Among anthropologists, notably Claude Levi-Strauss, the family and kinship structures is the basic unit of all social relationships. These relationships form communities that consist of lineages and family groups, hopefully in a context of social cooperation to promote social stability. Notwithstanding conflict that arise between and among family members and lineages, these social relationships endure, without which we cannot claim ourselves to be human.

During the pandemic, the family assumed a whole new level of significance. For those who lived as a whole family, togetherness went into overdrive. Never had family members spent as much face time as during the perennial lockdowns and endless variations thereof.

For diasporic families, digital platforms became the site of instant reunions. Much like our family. We rediscovered absentee members whose lives were taken over by time, travel and busy careers. For dispersed family members, the diaspora was an ongoing reality for nearly five decades until the virus and the lockdown wove a thread around us, and we found one another in digital space.

We traced the paths we trod across the decades, marvelled at each other's digital images splattered across the computer monitor, detecting the changes wrought by years of separation. We looked back, eager for updates, recounted the memories—all of them funny and pleasant, avoiding the grim subject of illness and infection. Family was fresh air.

Take Roberto (Boboy as we fondly called him), my US-born nephew trained in emergency medicine. While visiting for the Christmas holidays in 2003, Boboy wrote his application essay for medical school at NYU. Then, he was living and working in Los

Angeles as an Emergency Medical Technician (EMT). I advised him to write a 'get real' essay—stories on the ground with real people, the ones whom he took care of and gave him the motivation to pursue a medical degree. He zeroed in on a delivery while in the ambulance on the LA freeway. It was his first taste of emergency medicine: helping the mother urge an infant out of her pelvis in the back of an ambulance. The mother was Hispanic, and so language skills added to his early medical exposure. He got into medical school and decided to specialize in trauma surgery.

He liked stitching bodies, he said, something I found too gory for my taste as a social scientist. But he found pleasure in seeing his elbow and eyebrow stitches in perfect alignment as a kind of artwork. We have the same genes for art and science, but not the same proclivities in our chosen career paths.

That was eighteen years ago. Today, he is on the frontlines of the Physicians Regional Medical Center in Naples, Florida. During residency, Boboy received biohazard training as an intrinsic part of his specialization in emergency medicine.

'We knew how to don and doff hazmat suits,' he said, 'so it was essentially the same thing (as the PPE). Intubating patients is what all ER doctors have been trained to do since day one of the residency.' Since COVID was considered an emergency, Boboy hit the ground running from day one.

But in the early days of the pandemic, Boboy, together with the hospital staff, did not know what the prognosis was.

'I remember a couple of shifts where I would see a patient at the beginning of my shift, and their vital signs were normal. They had pneumonia but their oxygen levels were 99 or 100 per cent. We would prescribe them antibiotics and discharge them home,' he recalled.

Then the same patient would return later on in his shift or the next day. It's a 180-degree turn.

'Their oxygen levels were 70 per cent or lower and they looked horrible. We were told to intubate the patients and put them in the ICU.' Some of them would not leave the ICU except in a body bag. Those were the hardest scenes—moving from intake of patients through rapid treatment, then to lose them as the machine beeped and their heart monitor flatlined. There were far too many of those moments. It was a dreadful Florida winter.

Now deployed for over a year, Boboy talked about how things have changed. The frenzy had worn off. In 2021, the Spring-breakers who partied in Florida's beaches with all abandon had finally left. Some sense of normalcy had returned to the state and Boboy was relieved. The virus did not come roaring back despite carefree youngsters who threw caution to the wind.

For starters, he said he was intubating a smaller number of patients. Most of them would be sent home, suffering more from hypochondria or a simple allergy. His medical duties were confined to comforting them, dispelling worries, dispensing advice, filling out prescriptions. Most of all, there was an established medical routine and the frenzied experimentation with treatment was over.

So Boboy had more time for his hobbies and continuous upgrading of his sprawling house. He built an extensive playroom where he decompresses, he said. He spent hours spray-painting his toy warriors, got lost in the details of body armour and weapons, and the intricacies of colour hues and shades. His favourite ones were assembled into a diorama. The distraction took him away from the hospital scenes and his painting hobby sealed and insulated him from the pandemic world.

I didn't know very much about Boboy's career path over the last twenty or so years that separated us. He didn't come to Asia very often, and the pandemic eliminated all travel. A good ten years must have passed since I last saw him. During that time, he became a full-fledged adult of a sudden, seeming light years away from the essay-writing exercise in my third-floor bedroom in Manila when he was competing to enter graduate school. Over a decade behind him as a practising physician and a homeowner to boot, I could not help but think that in the blink of an eye, he is suddenly older, with all the trappings of adulthood: a medical licence, a home mortgage, a registered car. And I am ever closer to mortality.

But there is family to hold our fears and anxieties together. To dispel the lingering uncertainties of my recovery and fears of reinfection. To cushion the loneliness of solitary living which my brother faced for eighteen months when the pandemic separated him from his wife. She looked after their son as he underwent major back surgery in America, and got caught up in cancelled flights and locked-down airports. He learned to live alone after over three decades of marriage and near-constant togetherness. It was a painful adaptation to solitary living in one of the longest lockdown periods in the world. Zoom was his only recourse.

So, we flooded him with recipes so he could cook his meals; gave him tips on growing herbs in his condominium; urged him to go for a walk in the roof deck for daily exercise. And overall helped dispel the demons of depression. Our phone calls and text messages saw the gradual return of his insufferable humour. His corny jokes were a welcome relief, never mind that they were hardly funny. Every morning, we awoke to the ritual of 'Good Morning, Sunshines' in our sibling Viber group, a year-long pact that has yet to be broken. He was and still is, the digital rooster at dawn. His morning messages are as ubiquitous as the mobile phone that has become mandatory paraphernalia in the era of the pandemic.

'The virus brought out the best in all of us,' texted my sister-in-law over Viber, my brother's stranded wife, now reunited with him after eighteen months of waiting and two jabs of the Pfizer vaccine that finally brought her back home. Her flight over the Pacific was the most monitored in our family travel history, from the time she checked into the San Francisco Airport to her final disembarkation in Manila. Hers was a sixteen-hour journey that became everyone's obsession, the first one in our family in the age of COVID. While quarantined for ten days in Manila, we inquired about her hotel room, the food tray that was served and left at the doorstep, the neighbourhood delivery of her favourite snacks. When she finally stepped into her own home, firmly in the embrace of her husband, we, the conniving siblings shut him off from Viber for a few days. His reunion with her was so very well-deserved, like being rewarded with the sweetest sugary ice cream on a torrid summer day. And we let him enjoy the moment to the hilt without anyone of us peering into their private enjoyment.

Thus do we illustrate Durkheim's solidarity. We siblings, dispersed and separated by globalization, disrupted by the pandemic, found our interdependence and strengthened it. Sure, we disagreed and differed on the subject of running my mother's household via remote control. Long, oftentimes tedious Zoom discussions over salaries of caregivers, their sleeping schedules and allocation of tasks never lapsed into acrimony. We tamed the urge to quarrel and bicker even if we got lost in the minutiae of repairing the nearly dilapidated screen door and the clogged-up roof drainage when the monsoon season arrived. Mostly, it was fun. Lengthy discussions over the appropriate size and shape of my mother's pillows to help her sleep better were hilarious. We would pause the discussion on logistics to share interesting titbits of our daily, pandemic-driven lives, from gardening to online shopping.

Perhaps I over-romanticize. But two years of separation from my siblings and their respective families convinces me that our physical separation never diminished our affection for one another. We miss each other's presence for sure.

There is a preserved transcript of our WhatsApp messages in early April 2020 about the first day of my confirmed COVID-19 test. There was shared anxiety each day when I was in the hospital. The same shock when we learned that my sister's entire household was infected during the Christmas season in 2020. Each and every day was a mobilized family brigade of prayer warriors, storming the heavens to plead for our recovery. Over a period of eight months as the pandemic wore on, we all did recover. In that return to health was our family strengthened and held together which no virus could weaken. It is now just a matter of time, and the waiting looks promisingly shorter, when we can physically reunite and embrace each other again.

Chapter 14

The Legend of Maginhawa Street

I don't remember Maginhawa Street at all. I used to live in the general neighbourhood in the late 1980s when I was starting my academic career at the nearby University of the Philippines. The neighbourhood is well-known for its predominantly academic habitués and their soulmates in the non-profit sector. Living in this neighbourhood was like the Philippine version of the hippie communes in San Francisco in the 1960s.

The street faded with time, but Ana Patricia Non jogged my memory. Her famous bamboo cart during the lockdown was a makeshift, roadside, food pantry intended especially for the poor and the hungry residents nearby.

Maginhawa is a Filipino term that carries several meanings: cosy, easy, comfortable, convenient, restful, homely, reposeful, full of relief. In Cebuano, the largest major dialect in the Philippines spoken by some 20 million Filipinos, the term means 'breath'. Thus, in April 2021, when the community pantry on Maginhawa Street in Quezon City suddenly sprung up out of nowhere, there was, like the street's name, a breath of relief, a response, a sense of comfort and convenience.

People flocked to the pantry instantly. Early morning queues formed as early as 5 a.m. There was no lack of enthusiasm to donate food items from generous donors who viewed the pantry as an opportunity to be more positively engaged during the pandemic crisis. From Maginhawa Street, the initiative spread like wildfire all over the country, emulating the small experiment at collective action that began on a residential road. Ana Patricia Non, a twenty-six-year-old entrepreneur, was the initiator of the community pantry. She did not expect the widespread reaction to her donation of food which she posted on the sidewalk of Maginhawa Street: some rice, pasta, beans, salt, water, fresh vegetables. And a placard that read: 'give what you can, take what you need.'

'I am tired of complaining, I am tired of inaction. This is a gut issue,' she was quoted in an interview for a publication of The Lowy Institute in Australia. Her story travelled far and wide and she emerged as a kind of accidental heroine in a spontaneous, nationwide movement to feed those who were hungry and had limited access to food during the pandemic. But she was also driven by compassion for those who had lost their jobs, like her employees in her small furniture shop that shut down when lockdown hit Manila. It was then that she saw the difficulties her employees faced, from lost livelihoods to the simple inability to feed themselves.

On the eve of lockdown, Patricia rushed to a supermarket and bought a surplus of goods that clogged her place. She surveyed her flat and witnessed the outcome of her impulsive hoarding, while her television flashed images of poor people across the screen, without the wherewithal to shop before the night-time curfew, let alone accumulate excess food items.

That's when her disquietude began.

The following afternoon, Ana Patricia walked along the street of Maginhawa close to where she lived and searched for a spot that would accommodate sizeable foot traffic. She found a space fronting two commercial stores, approached the owners, and asked for permission to use the space for a community pantry. Permission granted, she rushed home and picked up the packed goods, and parked them in a bamboo cart. She hoisted a placard with a simple message of taking what one needed. Thus was born the legendary community pantry of Maginhawa Street.

Within minutes a queue of people had come to partake of the free food in the parked bamboo cart. Every single day, Patricia unwittingly found herself rising very early at dawn to replenish the food items and manage the donations that came in through her electronic account via her mobile phone.

Unexpectedly, the community-pantry idea overflowed outside of her street and spread to the provinces rather quickly, much to her own surprise. It did not take long for community pantries to sprout everywhere. Just like the COVID, community pantries exploded. Within the same month of its founding, there were 358 community pantries and several months later, about 6,700 community pantries were operating all over the country.

The Filipino sociologist, Randolf David, wrote in his weekly column on the charismatic appeal of the community pantry, and how it tapped into the trait of generosity. At its core, he wrote,

> . . . generosity is about anonymity and selflessness. Generous acts are bereft of all self-aggradizement and offer no space for the self-promotion and obligatory acknowledgments that usually accompany the mass distribution of emergency assistance.

Also, generosity elicits the ethical practice of taking. While the generous giver expects nothing in return, the taker must also practise patience and self-control. One must wait for one's turn to partake of the pantry and must only take what one truly needs. The temptation to hoard is all too real, yet for the spirit of the community pantry to continue and endure, both giver and taker must subscribe to the ethics of selfless giving and gracious receiving, so that both giver and taker can be further humanized.

Another Filipino scholar, Virgilio Enriquez, referred to the community pantry as the embodiment of *kapwa*, loosely translated as otherness, the practice of which binds both the self and the other into a psychic unity. A simple, bamboo cart loaded with food items tapped into the universal bond of humanity.

While the success of the community pantry foregrounded the positive features of Philippine culture, it also highlighted another glaring pandemic in the country: hunger.

It was hunger that animated the generosity of people like Ana Patricia Non, and the groundswell of her simple gesture. In the bamboo cart of her donated food items was hunger embedded. People flocked instantly to the cart in response to their immediate hunger, and their impatience at the government that had not, one year later, responded adequately to the gnawing in their stomachs and the continuing uncertainty in their lives. The community pantry, said Ana, was 'a response to famine.'

CNN Philippines did a coverage in May 2021 of the hunger crisis in the Philippines which the pandemic exacerbated. A family living in the Baseco compound, one of the poorest areas in urban Manila, houses about 60,000 people living in a cramped reclamation area, where people congregated to take advantage of economic opportunities around the dock site. The lockdowns however stopped all economic activity especially fishing which was a lifeline for many of its residents.

Taking her cue from Ana Patricia Non, Nadja de Vera organized a community kitchen in May 2021. She was shocked by the poverty she witnessed in the compound, she told CNN. Through donations from farmers and fishermen, de Vera distributed the food to whoever came to the Baseco community kitchen. For many of the compound's residents, the community kitchen became their only source of sustenance, especially during the lockdown.

One family, Mona Liza Vito, who has nine children and one grandchild, used to earn a living by peeling garlic and stuffing them into bags and earned about US$2 a day. With the lockdown, her work shut down and that of her husband in a construction site. The community kitchen provided free food for her family even if it was just for one full meal a day. She was grateful that their hunger was staved off through direct donations.

The reputable polling organization, Social Weather Station (SWS), reported that in September 2020, 30.7 per cent of Filipinos suffered hunger, and 8.7 per cent suffered severe hunger. Almost a year later in May 2021, a year after the imposition of the lockdown, over four million Filipinos, or about 16.8 per cent of the population reported having experienced hunger at least once in the past three months. The polling organization called it involuntary hunger defined as hunger because there was not enough to eat.

The World Health Organization estimated that more than 3 million children in the Philippines have stunted growth due to hunger and malnutrition. About 618,000 children were 'wasted', that is, their weight is very low compared to their height due to inadequate food and prolonged illnesses.

Globally, the situation wasn't any better. In fact, in many parts of the world, the situation was more dire than in the Philippines. World hunger spiked during the pandemic according to a joint publication in July 2021 by the Food and Agriculture Organization of the United Nations (FAO), the International Fund for Agricultural Development (IFAD), the United Nations Children's Fund (UNICEF), the United Nations World Food Programme (WFP) and the World Health Organization (WHO).

A tenth of the global population, up to 811 million people, were undernourished in 2020, said the report. A tenth of the global population suffered from

> . . . an uncomfortable or painful sensation caused by insufficient energy
> from diet.

Almost a billion people in 2020 suffered from food deprivation and from not eating enough calories. But the sharpest rise in hunger was in the African continent. An estimated 21 per cent of the entire population suffered from undernourishment, more than double of any other region.

Other statistics offered a bleak portrayal. In 2020, more than 2.3 billion people in the world lacked year-round access to adequate food, otherwise known as the prevalence of moderate or severe food insecurity. Women suffered more food insecurity than men: for every ten food-insecure men, there were eleven food-insecure women.

Children suffered the most in terms of malnutrition. In 2020, over 149 million children under five years old were estimated to suffer from stunted growth, that is, they were too short for their age. More than 45 million were stunted, or too thin for their height, yet ironically, nearly 39 million were overweight.

But it was not a food shortage problem, claimed the International Food Policy Research Institute (IFPRI) based in Washington. In its February 2021 report, IFPRI stated that the global food system was resilient enough to withstand the shocks caused by the pandemic. There was enough food supply to feed the whole world. So how does one explain this contradiction?

The answer, according to the Welthungerhilfe, the largest private-aid organization in Germany, was not due to lack of availability but rather due to lack of access. Those who had access to food did not suffer hunger during the pandemic. Typically, the wealthier countries who had the resources to secure food items, whether through domestic production systems or importation, experienced minimal disruption in their food supplies.

Whereas poorer countries especially those living in the rural areas bore the brunt of the pandemic. Lockdowns prevented their ability to obtain access to food sources. Farmers and fishermen suffered from restricted mobility and could not transport their produce, nor obtain inputs for their production systems. Those working in the informal sector, typically the urban poor who were street vendors and stall owners, closed down their shops and stayed home, unable to earn any income from their already meagre economic activities. Migrant workers stopped sending remittances home when financial systems temporarily closed down, leaving their overseas dependents in even more precarious conditions. Meanwhile, supermarkets and grocery stores managed to leverage their resources by shifting online and making tremendous profits. The poorer populations were mostly left to fend for themselves or wait for charitable donations and dole-outs.

The hungriest countries in the world suffer from a confluence of factors called the three Cs: conflict, climate change and COVID-19, according to Concern Worldwide, a global humanitarian organization founded in Ireland in 1968. Not surprisingly, the hungriest countries are those that are simultaneously experiencing conflict and political instability as in the examples of Yemen, the Democratic Republic of Congo (DRC) and Afghanistan. Other countries like Madagascar suffer from droughts while Chad is in the throes of both ethnic violence and weather extremes. Haiti, on the other hand, had just experienced another devastating earthquake in August 2020 even while the country was struggling with COVID-19. In these countries, undernourishment rates are very high: 47 per cent in Haiti, almost half of its entire population, 43 per cent in Madagascar and 32 per cent in Chad. To worsen matters, Chad hosts approximately 500,000 refugees from Sudan, the Central African Republic and Nigeria. Haiti's president was brazenly assassinated in July 2021, and the country deteriorated into anarchy as the population, already suffering from the pandemic and fuel shortages, had to deal with gang violence and kidnappings.

The hungriest country in the world is Somalia. According to www. besttourism.com, it is perhaps also the poorest country in the world, its economy the most underdeveloped. About half the population are nomads, and more than 50 per cent of its population have no registered place of residence. Those who are employed in the urban areas survive on no more than 40–50 dollars a month. The financial system has collapsed. Most children dream of becoming pirates as this is the only way to get money quickly.

Hunger in Somalia is a reflection and a result of simultaneous factors, chief of which is intractable conflict. Decades of conflict and political instability due to clan warfare and more recently, terrorism, have brought on endemic poverty and hunger. About half of the population, approximately 6 out of 12 million, suffer from food insecurity. A decade ago, in 2011, about a quarter-million Somalians died from famine. Because of poor rainfall and water shortage, about three-quarters of the country's livestock died, and droughts reduced maize and sorghum harvests by 25 per cent.

Even while COVID-19 mortalities were purportedly low in Somalia, it is estimated that the death rate is at least thirty-two times higher than reported figures. Undercounting and lack of data precision were due to the lack of a definitive registration system for deaths. These multiple problems plaguing Somalia seem almost unsolvable, prompting many observers and scholars to call it a failed state.

The UN joint report stated that solving the global hunger problem will require 'increased diplomatic momentum' because of the critical juncture brought about by COVID-19.

> This year offers a unique opportunity for advancing food security and nutrition through transforming food systems with the upcoming UN Food Systems Summit, the Nutrition for Growth Summit, and the COP26 on climate change.

Nearly two years into the pandemic, the world simply cannot afford to wait for the 'increased diplomatic momentum', at least not in terms of solving the immediate problem of hunger and the stark possibility of famine that many countries face.

Community pantries, food banks and community kitchens such as those begun by Ana Patricia Non and Nadja de Vera are stop-gap measures that respond to immediate needs. The bamboo carts provide food directly to the needy at critical moments when hunger is at the doorstep of many families. These initiatives stave off hunger today and tomorrow. They will continue even while their numbers have dropped off, in response to the lowered numbers of cases and as the country gradually reopens to allow businesses to function again. True, these efforts were unsustainable, but these were never meant to be long-term solutions.

Hunger is endemic, and the poor, the Bible says, shall always be with you. Organizations like Welterhungerhilfe and Concern Worldwide will continue their efforts that began decades earlier, to eradicate hunger and poverty, to ensure that

. . . everyone in the world can lead a self-determined life, free from
hunger and poverty.

This is Welterhungerhilfe's stated mission and vision. It believes that
hunger is the biggest solvable problem in the world, that it can, with its
partners, achieve Zero Hunger by 2030.

Reflecting on the stories of Ana Patricia Non, Nadja de Vera
and the nameless, tireless people working behind the humanitarian
organizations, I thought of my escapade with crackers and cheese in
the hospital in April 2020. I realized that I was never hungry, only that I
suffered from cravings. I never knew deprivation. The hospital served
me three substantial meals a day with bonus biscuits and milk tea in
the afternoons. If at all, I had an oversupply of food, more than my
measly appetite could accommodate while I fought to shed the virus
and recover from COVID.

Just like Ana Patricia's bamboo cart and Nadja's community
kitchen, I felt 'maginhawa'—comfortable, convenient, restful, homely,
relieved, reposeful. Within the confines of my hospital room, every day
was utmost care and generosity. And I knew I was going to live.

The community pantries have closed down in the Philippines. As
the economy reopened and food became more accessible, the roadside
carts and community kitchens ceased operations. But the enterprising
spirit of Ana Patricia Non lives on. Many other Patricia Nons will
emerge in due course. Their inspirational actions especially during
moments of global distress remind us of Abraham Lincoln's famous
aphorism:

Though passion may have strained, it must not break our bonds of
affection. The mystic chords of memory will swell when again touched,
as surely they will be, by the better angels of our nature.

Chapter 15

When God Went Viral

Prayerful, yes. Religious, no. I was never the latter, nor was I particularly observant about the religious practices of others. I am comfortable with my own private spirituality. But during the pandemic, religious behaviour exploded and there was no escaping religiosity as a daily facet of lockdown lives. Religion and the pandemic piqued my curiosity in a major way. I was born a Catholic after all, and I have never shed the cloak of spirituality even as I continue to resist religious rituals. As a sociologist, I thought of religiosity as a major social force, both constructive and destructive. There was no escaping God. During the pandemic, religion staged a massive comeback.

In my mother's home, there wasn't much going on for over two years. Three adopted dogs break the tedium of daily contact among five humans who constitute the totality of their human interaction. The well-fed and amply trained dogs chased after rats, insects and cockroaches to keep the house speckless. Theirs is an urban hermitage, smack in the middle of an upscale, gated community that could be construed as an almost perfect animal-human coexistence.

Thus, she prays, as hermits do in their caves of isolation. Communing with the spiritual has been her daily fare. Digital masses, neighbourhood novenas, YouTube sermons, Internet pilgrimages were her near constant companions. Hers was televised spirituality, a new form of worship that shifted God's location from the church to the ether.

Elsewhere in the world, where interaction did not grind to an absolute halt, religious rituals have sprung up almost instantly since the imposition of the lockdown among friends and family who have been kept apart by the coronavirus. Prayer groups formed in abundance overnight: to offer novenas for the sick, collectively invoke divine power to spare them from infection, pray and mourn for the dearly departed whom they have not had the chance to see and bid farewell to. Prayer occasioned kin- and friendship-renewal, a digital reaching-out across the globe to reconnect.

Over the past two years, news of family and friends who have passed away have been plentiful. I stopped counting. Each week there would be someone I knew who lost the battle against the virus. Or, having recovered, would yield to illnesses that have lain dormant, spurred to life by a viral assault that left them weakened and defenceless.

I attended countless Zoom and YouTube, live-streamed masses for dear, departed friends and relatives. In our Catholic tradition, we pray continuously for nine days, believing that the soul stays in this world outside its body before making the final journey into infinity. For nine days, we gather digitally to pray for the departed soul's smooth transition into the next life, cleansed by our prayers, elated by our eulogies and readied for the final phase of their passage into the light. As I write this piece in late 2021, our community of family and friends across the globe gathered at the same hour daily to pray for the repose of my cousin, whose passing a few days ago was unexpected and unnerving. It is a nine-day ritual that Catholics call the 'novena' at the end; we believe his soul will have been purged of all distorted energies and his spirit purified to merit his entrance into Heaven.

'Religion is a medium through which humans forge threads of connectedness,' wrote the sociologist, Dr Joseph MT, at the University of Mumbai in India. These threads can bind its adherents into a tight weave, as in close-knit religious communities, cults, or secret societies.

Or even when the congregation is loosely threaded, religion scoops and envelops its followers into a kind of oversized religious caftan. At no time are these threads more significant than during the pandemic, a period of physical separation and distance mediated most effectively by religion.

As the Christian philosopher, Lactantius (about 313 AD), asserted, the etymology of the word 'religion' is rooted in the Latin word 'ligare', meaning to bind. Later on, Augustine, purportedly the most celebrated father of the Latin Church, gave his assent to its meaning. Closely related is the English word 'ligament'—those fibrous elastic tissues that connect the bones and joints of human bodies and function as flexible, protective and stabilizing parts of our anatomy. Finally, Professor William Walter Skeat of the University of Cambridge and author of *An Etymological Dictionary of the English Language* stated that the word is derived from the old English term *reck*, meaning to 'heed' or to 'care for'. Embedded in these terms lie precise components of religion—a binding, heeding, caring force for people that constitutes a protective and stabilizing force, without which human society seems incomplete.

The functionality of religion came into sharp relief during the pandemic. When the secular realm came up short with answers and solutions, religious faith filled in the vacuum. Science seemed to be on the back foot for a long year while the world awaited the arrival of a vaccine. Cynics, critics, naysayers, agnostics and atheists viewed God's reappearance as a convenient time-filler.

Among the faithful, globally, a religious revival was underway. A Pew Research Center survey in April 2020 tracked changes in Americans' beliefs during the pandemic. Almost a quarter of Americans (24 per cent) said that the pandemic has strengthened their faith in contrast to 2 per cent who said their faith was weakened. The most significant change in religious belief was among Protestants in the historically black tradition, followed by Evangelicals, Catholics and mainline Protestants. Faith among Jews remained unchanged, while a small percentage of atheists (2 per cent) reported some change in their beliefs, although it is unclear whether the shift is towards more or less belief or more or less disbelief.

A year later in 2021, the Pew Research Center extended the survey to fourteen other countries. It reported a strengthening of religious faith in Spain, Canada and the United Kingdom during the pandemic. Across all fourteen countries, the increase in faith was overwhelmingly more significant than the people who said their religious faith had weakened. Those with lower incomes considered religion an important aspect of their lives and reported that the pandemic had strengthened their faith. Where there is adversity, God is not far behind.

Religious practice is perhaps the most outward manifestation of adaptation to the pandemic. Faith, after all, is sustained through rites and rituals which social scientists term the performative aspect of religion. According to sociologist Emile Durkheim, ritualistic practices enable 'collective efflorescence' in his celebrated work on *The Elementary Forms of Religious Life*. When people come together in groups to communicate the same thought and repeatedly practise the same gestures of worship, the group unites and individuality disappears. There is only unity with one another and with God, or with the gods. Raised hands, swaying bodies, loud penetrating voices are high-octane activities that transform the congregation into a sacred gathering in which people infect each other with their crowd-sourced divinity.

But lockdowns closed many places of worship, collective efflorescence had to be sought elsewhere. Technology was the obvious answer to this religious quandary. Two Filipino theologians, Justine Renus Galang and Willard Enrique Macaraan, wrote about creating a new 'agora' via social media platforms. As in ancient Greece where the agora was 'the heart of the city for dialogue, trade, and worship', the same concept and practice would guide the Catholic church in the pandemic era. The Catholic Pope Francis seized on the power of social media through live broadcasts of global rosary prayers in May 2020 on YouTube, a live-streamed message and blessing during Christmas 2020, a global broadcast of his first trip to Iraq where he met with the top Shia Muslim clerics in Najaf, and issued a plea for finding common ground among different faiths. Stamping one's leadership in the realm of organized religion required one to be social-media savvy.

Because no virus can prevent religion from denying its performative dimension, believers quickly improvised and reinterpreted worship through alternative avenues of worship. Dr Carola Lorea at the Asia Research Institute at the National University of Singapore founded the blogsite *CoronAsur: Religion and COVID-19* to document some of the ingenious adaptations during the early days of the pandemic. Among them are live-streamed Zoom concerts of the Baul religious community in India, the proceeds and donations went to deliver groceries and essential goods to the itinerant singers; the payment of *zakat* (charity/almsgiving) in Indonesia through mobile phone apps, with a sharp increase in payment transfers during the Ramadan; the practice of *prasad* in which food is packaged and sanitized for devotees to pick up at the Hindu temples. Then there's 'liturgical televisuality' in the predominantly Catholic Philippines, which, according to Filipino assistant professor Louie Sanchez, picked up pace during the lockdown and mobilized not only liturgical services but also financial support for the upkeep of churches. The only Catholic television, the TV Maria, aired masses and religious services during the Lenten week that coincided with the lockdown imposition. As digital religious worship became the norm over the year, YouTube and Facebook live-streamed many masses, rosary recitations and the digital exposition of religious figures and icons; the Manila Cathedral, considered the most 'polished' liturgical televisuality on Facebook, generated an initial following of 40,000. Over the pandemic year, the number swelled to 400,000 followers. Even religion has to have a good, social-media strategy.

The *Hajj* pilgrimage to Saudi Arabia in 2020 was a motley crowd of about 1,000 pilgrims. In any given year before the pandemic, attendees would swell up to 2 million. For the first time, international travellers were banned from coming to the holy cities of Mecca and Medina. By the time of the pilgrimage, Saudi Arabia reported 270,000 cases and 2,700 deaths. The Hajj would be the smallest and the most physically distanced ever, a dramatically far cry from the pressed bodies of past pilgrimages. In 2021, the expedition went digital. 'Hajj cards' were rolled out, allowing pilgrims contactless access to religious sites, accommodation and transport. Colour-coded plastic cards assisted pilgrims through the different stages of the Hajj. They received sanitized stones for the ritual 'stoning of the devil' as the last significant ritual of the pilgrimage. The Saudi authorities provided the stones in sealed bags, each one containing seven stones. Digitalization facilitated the movement of massive numbers and afforded crowd control. Stampedes and accidents were avoided. Still and all, only 60,000 pilgrims who were already residents in the kingdom and were vaccinated, were allowed to make the pilgrimage. They were chosen through a digitalized lottery system, and all transactions were electronic. Overseas pilgrims were banned for a second year. The foremost attraction was the deployment of robots that distributed *Zamzam* (holy) water to the pilgrims instead of communal dispensers. 'In the future, the Hajj will become a contactless event,' said Mr Amro al-Maddah, undersecretary at the Hajj Ministry, and the hajj cards will serve as virtual wallets for payments.

Throughout the digital space, the pandemic provided an occasion to link it with religious worldviews including the Apocalypse, the so-called 'end times' when the day of judgement has finally come upon humanity. A website called End Times Truth predicted the second coming of Jesus the Messiah. Quoting from the gospels of the apostles Matthew and Luke, the end times refers to the 'beginning of sorrows' purportedly from the words of Jesus himself:

> And ye shall hear of wars and rumours of wars: see that ye be not troubled: for all these things must come to pass, but the end is not yet. For nation shall rise against nation, and kingdom against kingdom: and there shall be famines, pestilences, and earthquakes in divers(e) places. All these are the beginning of sorrows.

The apostle Luke in the Christian Bible is quoted as well:

> And great earthquakes shall be in divers(e) places, and famines, and pestilences; and fearful sights and great signs shall there be from heaven.

And from the Book of Ezekiel (38:22),

> I will plead against him with pestilence and the blood.

Last, there's the Book of Revelation 21:1, the final book in the New Testament of the Christian Bible, an influential book of prophecy, the authoritative source of all apocalyptic narratives. It was written by John the Elder (also believed to be John the Apostle) sometime around 95 AD while he was in exile on the island of Patmos off the west coast of present-day Turkey. His exile was the result of anti-Christian persecution under the Roman emperor, Domitian. The title of the book of Revelations comes from the Greek word 'apocalypse' which refers to the disclosure of something as yet unknown. The book did not disappoint. In hundreds of pages, it reveals how human existence will end, the methods that will accomplish the final purge and then the restoration of a purified humanity.

In the final four chapters of the Book of Revelation (19–22) is the triumphant arrival of Jesus Christ. The world is created anew for those who have been redeemed.

> Then I saw a new heaven and a new earth, for the first heaven and the
> first earth had passed away, and there was no longer any sea.

There is hope. However, there must also be repentance.

The book occupies a central place in Christian eschatology. Michael F. Bird, lecturer in theology at Ridley Melbourne College of Mission and Ministry, explains eschatology as the 'study of last things' and includes themes like Jesus' second coming, the events pertaining to before and after Jesus's return, questions about hell and the new creation. But the study is also devoted to what happens while the second coming has not yet happened as humanity awaits the full return of the Messiah.

Enter COVID-19. In the small Israeli town of Safed, chief rabbi and president of the Rabbinical Community Association, Shmuel Eliyahu, a hard-line, right-wing religious leader, preached that the coronavirus is a punishment from God and a sign of the coming of the Messiah. Quoted in the *Jerusalem Post* in the early days of the outbreak, he announced:

> The Jewish people live, we are waking up, opening our eyes, stopping all
> the nonsense we do, and drawing closer to Shabbat.

Echoing rabbi Eliyahu are rabbis Aviner and Mazuz, both of whom
decry human arrogance and haughtiness, post-modernism and moral
relativism, the LGBTQ community and Gay Pride marches. The latter
were events believed to have caused the outbreak. COVID-19 is the
summoning of humanity to repent and redeem itself. This theme would
be repeated throughout the pandemic. The Internet has been massively
populated with apocalyptic posts that linked the virus to Christian
eschatology and the means and methods by which redemption could
be obtained.

Apocalyptic narratives and pandemics 'run closely together',
according to Simon Dein at Queen Mary College at the University of
London. There has been recourse to religious explanations throughout
history, for example, during the Black Death in 1347–1352 and the
1918 Spanish flu. Humans committing sins figured prominently
in these narratives, so do moral transgressions like gay parades and
swinging couples—a kind of modern-day version of Sodom and
Gomorrah. These events supposedly awakened the four horsemen of
the Apocalypse as foretold in the Book of Revelation.

The first horseman, called Pestilence, rides a white horse. Vicente
Blasco Ibanez's novel, written in 1916, portrayed the horseman as

> . . . clad in a showy and barbarous attire. While his horse continued
> galloping, he was bending his bow to spread Pestilence abroad. At his
> back swung the brass quiver filled with poisoned arrows, containing the
> germs of all diseases.

Meant as a novel to illustrate the 'agony of humanity' that unleashed
the four horsemen, the story recounted the events of the 'tribulation',
reminiscent of the Book of Revelation, conjuring a time of judgement
for those left on earth after the 'rapture'.

Christian Evangelicalism is replete with rapture references.
However, the Evangelical world is totally alien to me. Thus, I scrounged

through Google to educate myself. Joshua Rivera, an 'evangelical kid' as he refers to himself, explained it eloquently in a piece entitled 'Vanished from the Earth', May 2021, published in an online magazine called *The Slate*:

> The idea of the rapture emerged from the biblical Book of Revelation, in which St. John has an elaborate apocalyptic vision that eventually ends with Christ's victory over evil. Thus the rapture warns of a terrible period for humanity in the lead-up to the end of all things, full of suffering, war, and natural disaster like we've never seen before. At its core, the rapture is a promise that you will not be here to witness all of that chaos and darkness. Christ will come back to collect the true believers still alive on earth—hence the familiar cultural imagery of slumped piles of clothes and cars abandoned in the street as believers are snatched away in an instant—to unite them in Heaven with the other believers who have already reached the end of their natural life. Everyone else gets to find out how bad things can really get here on earth, as our species marches to oblivion.

If I understood the previous passage correctly, these left-over humans would suffer immensely through the tribulation period. And when they are all cleansed through long-standing suffering, they will be spiritually laundered and 'whisked' up and away into the heavens. Then the second return of the Messiah can finally take place, as the arrival of the last main course—the pièce de résistance—in an endless buffet of mediocre dishes that one had to labour through. Finally, the Messiah returns in a blaze of glory. By the way, he will also most likely be male and White, and he will arrive in America, of course. No one knows when it will happen, only that it will. America will resurrect as a White male Christian nation—what Evangelicals have always believed America should be. Let me quote from Joshua Rivera again, for he put it rather brutally:

> Pastors from Franklin Graham to Cary Gordon have worked to make the evangelical faith synonymous with their domestic agenda: the preservation of white supremacy and minority rule, the continued privatization of the

public sector, the continued marginalization of the LGBTQ community, and victory in the never-ending culture wars . . . And the whiteness of evangelism gets laundered through ideas like good old-fashioned values, patriotism, and bootstraps capitalism . . . Evangelicalism is defined in the public imagination by a horde of loud, crusading white men looking to extend their own political and cultural clout. But it's also something else. For some, in fact, the less power you have, the more you believe, and the more faith you cling to; the more poverty you face, the less room you have in your heart, your mind, to trace the structures of power.

Enamoured by this rather profound and disturbing theological concept, I resorted to YouTube to complete this research and writing experience, to obtain an audio account combined with a written one. I wanted to hear, not only read, about the rapture. Since the outbreak, YouTube has likewise been replete with streamlined sessions of numerous pastors who explained COVID-19 in terms of the apocalypse. Here are a few notables:

Dr Ed Hindson of the First Redeemer Church explained the 'seven prophetic end-time promises' for a full forty-five minutes. First promise:

The promise of the rapture is the first of those seven promises. That when the Lord returns, when he comes back in the clouds (sic), he is coming back for his own initially. He's not comin' for everybody. He's comin' for those who know him as savior.

And by the way, Dr Hindson also promoted his book *Future Glory: Living in the Hope of Rapture, Heaven and Eternity*. Well, why not? Preach fear and earn royalties at the same time.

Jeff Jackson, also of the First Redeemer Church, talked about the signs of the end times. They are as follows: the re-gathering of the Jews via the state of Israel; moral inversion or moral relativism; and globalism. The most important question of the end of times is already upon the world: are you ready for the end?

Getting ready for the end times entails nothing more nor less than acknowledging Jesus as Saviour and living one's life according to the central precepts of Evangelical Christianity. In addition, one has to be prepared, says the Evangelical pastors, to be ready for the Lord's return.

> Be ready for Jesus to come take His bride to Heaven . . . He wants to find His bride ready and pure at His return.

Central to the end times is the anti-Christ. The drama is not complete without him. Yes, he is male. Jeff Kinley of the First Redeemer Church summed up who he is, according to more than 100 passages in the scriptures. He is just about the most prominent figure of the end times besides Jesus Christ. Thirty-six references in the Bible refer to him as the Beast. According to Pastor Jeff, the anti-Christ will have a wild, ravenous quality about him, seeking those he may devour. His characteristics, all backed up in the scriptures, are the following: an ambitious politician, a military demagogue, interested in power and not in women, only in power (Pastor Jeff: 'some surmised he may even be a homosexual'), a master orator, charming, cunning, deceptive, arrogant, lawless, blaspheming and a Jew-hater. The anti-Christ will lead and rule a ten-nation coalition, the members of which are reconstituted from the former Roman empire. This revived empire will be the world government. The pen of the anti-Christ will sign a peace treaty with Israel, but this will usher in the seven-year tribulation period. That is supposedly predicted in the Book of Daniel 9:27. The vaccine, said Pastor Jeff, is not the mark of the beast.

Those not jumping on the apocalypse bandwagon resorted to self-help measures as a way of easing the torment of lockdown. In the early days when no cure was available, and the number of infected cases rose globally, religion behaved like badly-wanted comfort food. In March 2020, with many states under lockdown, a website called the *Daily Signal* featured fifteen pastoral leaders across the US, each offering their advice on using the time wisely and retaining hope amid extreme uncertainty. The free flow of online counselling included several exciting proposals: practise silence in the tradition of the Desert Fathers, a community of third-century monks; make schedules for a recreational time during quarantine; read and remember history, especially the Christians in ancient Rome during the period 249 AD to 262 AD when up to 5,000 people died due to the plague (so, therefore, be grateful!); take long walks; write encouraging messages on your sidewalk; love your neighbours, literally, by starting a Zoom prayer meeting and read the Bible, preferably the Book of Ephesians every day for two weeks. My favourite was: check-in with each other and ask the question: 'How is it with your spirit?' to which the other should respond: 'Reclaiming Hallelujah!'

Having heard more than I intended to about Christian Evangelicalism, feeling discombobulated by this astounding worldview I had never encountered, I recalled my past predilections for music and remembered a song that had a similar title. So, I punched the search keys, and there it was: the sultry singer Anita Baker sings 'Caught up in the Rapture of Your Love.' 8.1 million views on YouTube in 2014, another 5.68 million views in 2015. 'Makes me want to shut out the world and float on a cloud of relaxation.' Sounded like she and her lover have already been whisked and raptured right here on earth.

The live version of some fifteen years ago showed her strutting onstage in a white flouncy skirt. The gossamer material floated about as she twirled twice onstage, clapped her hands, waved to the ecstatic crowd, grabbed the microphone, cued the band and the back-up singers, and launched in a full, throaty, smoky voice the opening lines of the song:

> When we met, I always knew,
> I would feel the magic of you.

She shimmied in her white high heels as she belted out some more:

> I want you in my life for all ti-i-i-ime.

She did know more about rapture as love, longing and desire, whether for God or another human, or both. The kind that most humans, I dare say, would prefer to experience and carry in their hearts, especially if indeed the end times are near.

Chapter 16

Toilet-paper Wars and the Rise
of the 'Sovereignists'

Toilet paper was never on my mind. I had the virus to worry about and my singular focus was my immune system. Besides, there was always an ample supply of toilet paper in my hospital bathroom. Until I read about toilet-paper shortages in the *New York Post* in early April 2020 and the contentiousness that these shortages generated in many parts of the world, this story was pure comic relief.

Very early on, when the lockdown was imminent in many parts of the world, fights broke out in supermarkets over panic buying. The Singapore *Straits Times* reported in March 2020 about a tussle in a Sydney supermarket over toilet paper. Cameras recorded three women pulling each other's hair, screaming and struggling over the coveted commodity. Police were called in to restore calm.

'It's not *Thunderdome*, it's not *Mad Max*,' said acting inspector Andrew New from New South Wales, referring to the post-apocalyptic films that were both set in a future dystopian vision of Australia. It's not *Mortal Kombat* either, the popular video game of assassins, recently franchised and converted into a movie, released just a year after the outbreak.

What has toilet paper, perpetual combat and dystopia have to do with each other? You might ask.

'It's our sense of heightened scarcity,' said health economist Dr Farasat Bokhari of the University of East Anglia in Britain, quoted in the Bangkok Post.

> My guess is we want to feel in control, and we have limited budgets . . .
> (s)o we go buy something that is cheap to buy, that we can store, and we
> know at the back of our minds that we are going to use anyway.

It's all about risk management. Humans are wired to eliminate risk, and toilet paper, being easy, cheap and superficial, is preferred to something more costly.

The other item is instant noodles. Same argument. Available, affordable. And mostly convenient. A hot cup of water will do the trick, and a few tubs of those high-calorie carbos will fill one's stomach quickly. The perfect comfort food.

On the other hand, no one quarrels over caviar. Too elaborate to prepare. The net satisfaction is possibly far too low to make it worth the effort. Those pesky, minute, fish eggs, if inappropriately served, might tumble on to the carpet. Besides, nobody gets stuffed on caviar. During lockdown, who cares about status binge-ing?

Scarcity theory has been around longer than this pandemic. Some eighty years ago, Lionel Robbins, the British economist, widely recognized as the father of scarcity theory, asserted that humans' demand for certain goods and services far outstrips their supply. Land, oil and gold are often-used examples. The competition for these goods intensifies when the population increases. Today, in the face of an expanding global population, water, once considered an abundant free resource, has been added to the list of increasingly scarce commodities.

If the theory holds, toilet-paper demand is unlimited, but supply is inadequate. Perceived as a commodity in short supply, the ruckus that ensued in pursuing this precious item is all but understandable, nonetheless unnecessary. There was no shortage of toilet paper in

Australia after all, but rationing followed after the altercation. Just to ensure that hoarding stopped, and no one was deprived.

That's just toilet paper. What there has been no shortage of is bad behaviour.

How about the passenger in a US airline who stuck a piece of gum and a lollipop on the passenger's hair in front of her who kept flipping her long hair behind the seat. Her overflowing locks blocked the screen of the passenger seated behind. The lady with the golden locks upfront seemed clueless to the goings-on behind her. Uploaded on TikTok, it was viewed 115 million times. The enjoyment of the gum-and-lollipop sticker was probably equal to the delight of the TikTok viewers.

CNN-USA reported that the unruly behaviour in airplanes was on the rise. The Federal Aviation Authority reported that since January 2021, there were more than 5,200 cases of bad behaviour among passengers. Unfortunately, imposing steep fines as high as US$24,000 didn't seem to work. Instead, flight crews, particularly women attendants, were often at the receiving end.

On the humorous side, three clueless campers boiled chicken in the hot springs at the Yellowstone National Park sometime in August 2020. The park ranger discovered the three wayward men and reported them to the authorities. They were banned from entering the park for two years, plus given fines of $500 to $1,200. That amount could buy a lot of chickens. The three men had 'cooked their own goose', quipped the retired Yellowstone historian Lee Whittlesey as reported to Todd Wilkinson in the UK newspaper the *Guardian*. But Alex Fox of the *Smithsonian* magazine added that the three men managed to eat the sulphur-boiled chicken and declared that, 'It was fantastic.'

Shafliq Alkhatib of the Singapore *Straits Times* reported that in the middle of lockdown in 2020, an elderly Singaporean man was said to have hurled vulgarities at a policeman and spat at another officer after being reminded to wear a mask.

It would have been infuriating if it weren't also so funny, often, just exasperating.

Why do people misbehave, especially during a pandemic? What prompts these anti-social behaviours? One would think, given this persistent virus that afflicts us all, no exceptions, would unify us into cooperation if only to beat this scourge. Not quite so.

One explanation, according to New York-based psychologist Sanam Hafeez is heightened levels of anxiety. The human race has been subjected to enormous strain for the past two years. And though progress has been achieved through the global roll-out of vaccines in late 2020, the uncertainty remains. Moreover, we all know that science, despite best efforts and record-breaking achievements, has not succeeded in eradicating the virus. Thus, our anxieties and our fears continue, and these two emotions feed on each other.

In an academic journal aptly titled *Anxiety, Stress and Coping*, two anxiety theorists Maria Miceli and Cristiano Castelfranchi, pointed out the close relationship between these emotions. Fear and anxiety, they argued, correlate with the threat of injury. Anxiety arises when humans lose pragmatic and epistemic control. The first (fear) refers to the loss of power over events, and the second (anxiety) refers to the inability to foresee what will happen. The pandemic exacerbated both human of these emotions.

Furthermore, both Miceli and Castelfranchi elaborated on the differences between fear and anxiety although there is a co-dependent relationship between these two emotions. While one might be anxious about toilet-paper shortage, there is no fear that the deprived person will die if toilet paper runs out. Anxiety is more diffuse: one can be anxious for a hundred reasons without any precise reason. Like running out of toilet paper.

People's concerns are of a wide range—from writer's block (which happens to me intermittently) to athletic performance. Fear, on the other hand, is more focused. The emotion has a goal: financial bankruptcy, homelessness, death from infection.

During the pandemic, both emotions moved into full gear. At the start of the pandemic, anxieties were heightened as the virus travelled across every continent. Hoarding was a stress response. It took a mere few weeks for governments to step up measures and assume greater control over the daily lives of their citizens. From anxiety, fear set in as the world settled into a mode of unpredictability as to when the pandemic might end. We moved from practical anxiety to existential fear. Though toilet-paper wars ended, fear of the unknown began.

Back to our misbehaving passengers and Yellowstone campers. Theirs might *not* be a case of anxiety or fear but rather of what sociologists call deviant behaviour. Deviance is a niche topic among social scientists who view society through the lens of harmony, stability and equilibrium. Deviance happens when we have all been de-stabilized and our balance deeply disturbed. Harmonious relations are the furthest thing from the minds of suffering humans who have been subjected to constraints of every form and measure, previously unimaginable. Unfortunately, deviant behaviour during a pandemic is too tempting to resist, and some have yielded to the seduction of once-in-a-while mischief.

A movie called *Lockdown* celebrated deviance light-heartedly. Filmed in London in July 2020 during the city's lockdown, it was a romantic comedy about a couple forced to postpone their breakup due to the coronavirus. They re-evaluated their relationship as they plotted to steal a three-million-pound diamond parked in the vault of Harrods. A duplicate diamond was safely smuggled into the vault while the real one was immersed in a fish tank surrounded by fake coral and plastic aquatic plants. The precious gem had to be inconspicuous. The very talented Anne Hathaway played Linda, the film's heroine. She was the CEO of a fashion company, and her boss requested her to clear inventory at the world-famous Harrods store. She also had the unpleasant task of firing several employees, many of them of long-standing service, via Zoom. Her husband, Paxton, played by the equally talented Chiwetel Ejiofor, was a driver of high-value deliveries who couldn't get a better job because of a previous, minor misdemeanour. Their relationship was all the more stressed with the pandemic, but they were exhilarated at the thought of theft under quarantine. So, they connived to steal the real diamond for themselves through an elaborate diamond-switching plot. The fake diamond was sent to the anonymous buyer (an unnamed, unsavory member of upper crust society) in New York City. The successful escapade did marvels for their relationship. The marriage spark returned. Though a tad unconventional, some inconsequential deviance is the best marriage therapy. Harmless mischief, a bit of fun to break the monotony of over-togetherness and lockdown-induced stress. But only in the movies, assuming the hapless buyer didn't discover the worthless duplicate.

The French sociologist, Emile Durkheim, coined the term 'anomie' which literally means 'without norms'. The term referred to a state of disruption during the nineteenth century in Europe when society was in transition from an agrarian to an industrial life. Durkheim wrote explicitly about the demise of intimacy and communalism in self-contained, close-knit communities and the rise of anonymity and isolation in assembly line factories in industrial society. A society in a state of anomie experiences a breakdown of the old standards of behaviour while the new values and norms are still being developed—a kind of time lag between one's current behaviour and one's previous beliefs. In this liminal space that the sociologist, Lewis Coser, describes as 'relative normative disorder', severe expressions of anomie could result in fatalism, a sense of futility and even suicide. All these are negative psychological consequences of the sudden social transformation which Durkheim observed during the Industrial Revolution in Europe.

The American sociologist, Robert Merton, borrowed Durkheim's concept of anomie to develop Strain Theory. He was interested in the phenomenon of crime in America. He argued that strain occurs when there is a disjuncture between individual goals, aspirations and expectations and the socially sanctioned means to obtain them. The typical example is the aspiration to acquire wealth and status. Because of the lack of social opportunities, individuals oftentimes cannot achieve these goals. Under stress, they have five choices as a response: conformity, innovation, ritualism, retreatism and rebellion.

In the pandemic context, we are all living through a severe disjuncture. Schools, offices and businesses have shut down. We stayed home. The place that was once our private sanctuary became the office, the school, the playground. The intimate domestic realm that previously shielded us from the competitive world transformed into a kind of everyday obstacle course. Our public and private needs and desires collided. Those with ample home space went into immediate zoning to demarcate their on and offline lives. But the more unfortunate ones who lived in cramped, urban quarters experienced spatial collision. Computer monitors overtook the dining table while children bounced around. Students on home-learning grabbed Internet connections from one another. In the absence of a playbook on cultural expectations during a pandemic, we all flirted with the temptation to deviate.

At the first taste of relative freedom, when lockdowns were lifted, and people could board a plane again or take a walk outdoors, the world seemed vaguely normal even while the virus lurked. But normalcy hasn't quite returned, and the new standards of behaviour were not yet fully developed. So why not boil chicken in a national reserve park (innovation), or stick gum in someone's hair (rebellion)? Some others embraced lockdown and celebrated the everyday humdrum of life in a bedroom (retreatism). In contrast, others dutifully wore masks to the grocery store to buy toilet paper without hoarding (conformity). Ritual practices, especially of the religious kind, became a daily feature in many homes whose inhabitants had time on their hands and an abiding belief that prayer could kill the virus and end the pandemic.

Yet another twist to the growing number of sordid tales under stress were claims of 'personal sovereignty' as the new form of resistance to stringent measures. In May 2020, the Singapore *Straits Times* ran a story about a forty-one-year-old woman who flouted the mask rule, claiming she was a 'sovereign' and the state had no jurisdiction over her. At an altercation with someone at the grocery store over her unmasked face, the woman responded that she didn't need to follow the rules because, in her words:

> I have nothing to do with the police, it means I have no contract with the police. They have no say over me. That's the thing. I'm not a person, I'm 'we the people'.

A year later, another story surfaced about a thirty-nine-year-old Briton, previously a resident in Singapore, who also claimed to be a sovereign. In May 2021, Channel News Asia reported that he was caught on video

while on the subway, refusing to wear a mask because 'rules don't apply'
to him. He also talked loudly to other commuters, saying,

> . . . I'm very religious and I love human beings. I hate seeing uncles,
> grandads with the mask on.

Several rounds of court hearings during which he showed up without a
mask resulted in his deportation in August 2021.

Complete control over one's body is the tip of the argument—a
kind of pro-choice stance in the battle over facial masks and social
distancing. So-called sovereigns argue that their body is not subject
to the dictates of the state. These are, to them, infringements on their
physique that the state does not have a right to. In many European
countries, protests against pandemic measures have been couched
in terms of personal autonomy and individual rights against states'
sovereign power. The website *OpenDemocracy* reports that right-wing
groups in Germany, Austria, Italy and Poland protested against
state officials who attempted to enforce restrictions on individual
behaviour and mobility in the face of the COVID-19 pandemic.
Even New Age and natural-health proponents have jumped on the
bandwagon of

> . . . bodily autonomy and bodily rights—the locus around which to
> contest the pandemic powers of the state.

Joseph Wilhelm, founder and CEO of the Rapunzel Naturkost AG
company that has been at the forefront of organic food in Germany
for four decades, invoked the sovereignists' claim to bodily rights when
he stated that

> . . . viruses are part of the earth's biological life.

Yes, rolling my eyes.

A focus on individual agency and responsibility, *OpenDemocracy* asserted, is a

> ... denial of public health as a collective good (and responsibility).

The 'responsibilization' of the individual even extended to other groups like anti-vaxxers and right-nativists movements who coalesced around the broad umbrella of 'sovereignists'—a new term that has entered the pandemic discourse.

Although a minority movement in several countries across the globe, the sovereignists have been resisting mitigation measures against the virus and believe the pandemic to be a hoax. In August 2020, the BBC carried a special coverage on the sovereign movement, detailing its spread to Canada, Australia and all across Europe. The FBI views the movement as 'domestic terrorism' and considers its followers as

> ... anti-government extremists who believe that even though they reside physically in this country, they are separate or 'sovereign' from the United States.

These statements would not have been too problematic except for the potential for violence. For example, a man claiming to be a sovereignist beheaded his landlord over a rental dispute in the US. He claimed to be immune from prosecution because of his status as a sovereignist.

The sovereign citizens' movement (SCM) has its roots in America, beginning in the 1970s. According to the Southern Law Poverty Center based in Montgomery, Alabama, the movement members believe that they should decide which laws to comply with and which ones to ignore. Wikipedia identified Gale William Potter, a Christian-identity minister, as the founder of the Posse Comitatus Movement in 1971. *The Nizkor Project* website describes the movement as a

> ... loosely organized group of 'Christian identity' activists ...

who believe that governmental power resides at the county and not at the federal level. Posse Comitatus is a Latin term that means 'power of the county'. The county sheriffs according to the movement's members are the highest governmental authority.

The sovereign movement is racist and anti-Semitic. Members believe that Jews have a plot to take over the world and that non-Whites were sub-human 'mud races'. Furthermore, they believe that Jews control governments.

In his master's thesis in 2016, Devon M. Bell investigated the SCM movement systematically. He traced its beginnings and its evolution. At its core, the SCM is an anti-governmental movement even if its origins were racist. Lothrop Stoddard, once of the movement's early ideologues, claimed the superiority of the Aryan (White) race and that racial variations were 'manifestations of impurities and therefore inferior.'

In later years, other racial groups embraced the SCM ideology, including African Americans, Asian Americans, Latinos and Jewish people. In July 2021, the *Washington Post* reported that a group of men who claimed to be members of the Rise of the Moors was charged with unlawful possession of weapons and ammunition. The arrested men claimed that as African Americans, they were descendants of African Moors and therefore had special rights based on a 1780s treaty with Morocco. Although living in the United States, they claimed to have the authority to detach themselves from the United States. The group is considered one of twenty-five active, anti-government, sovereign, citizen groups that the Southern Poverty Law Center identified in 2020.

SCM tactics involve 'paper terrorism', the practice of filing nuisance lawsuits and liens against personal property, resistance to paying taxes, filing administrative papers like insurances and driver's licences and even outright violence against government officials. SCM followers are self-proclaimed freemen and separatists. According to Devon Bell, the core of their belief is a rejection of the federal system and the acceptance of common law alone. Sovereignists believe that America's founding fathers set up a common law legal system but was secretly replaced by admiralty law, the law of the sea and international commerce. This swap of legal systems supposedly occurred during the Civil War or in 1933 when the United States abandoned the gold standard. Whatever the beliefs in this bogus history lesson, as the Southern Law Poverty Center calls it, sovereignists believe that judges and lawyers are foreign agents who are complicit in hiding the 'borrowed' and illegitimate character of the government. Therefore, sovereignists have a right to resist all aspects of this purportedly hidden and fraudulent government.

Unlike the mild mischievousness of the boiled chicken adventurers in Yellowstone National Park, the sovereignists' version of deviant behaviour is alarming. A belief deeply rooted in some twisted notion of individual rights and personal freedom is far more dangerous than a pandemic jerk acting out of frustration and boredom. The latter's problem is relatively easier to solve through self-care and community support, both of which are never in short supply. Even toilet-paper protagonists can be handled through proper rationing and better logistical management. But twisted ideologies? That's worse than a rampaging virus.

I remembered a brief discussion I had with my attending physician who, during one of his morning visits, assured me that my lungs had normalized and I was well on my way to recovery. However, I was still testing positive. I hadn't shed my viral load completely. He understood my anxiety and impatience. Over two weeks in the hospital was driving me stir crazy and I missed my husband, my bathroom and my own bed. Plus, I was starving of home-cooked food. But he put it rather succinctly: 'You are still a public-health risk. That's why we have to keep you here.' His gentle assertiveness shut me up. I didn't need any further explanation.

Chapter 17

Racism: The Other Pandemic

Racism, for me, is up close and personal. Having lived overseas for over twenty years, I had become sensitive to racism, even as nuanced language or covert behaviour. Someone at a dinner party once asked me if I was 'Filipina-Filipina'. Decoded: 'Are you a maid? Shouldn't you be scrubbing my floors instead?' Or looked askance at me and my Caucasian husband, probably trying to guess in which mail-order-bride magazine he had found me.

Google the terms 'racism' and 'pandemic', and you get about twenty-three pages and 271 entries. Most prominent is Fiona Godlee's blog entitled 'Racism: The Other Pandemic', which was featured in the *BMJ* website, a London-based medical journal dedicated to providing knowledge and expertise to improve healthcare outcomes. Since its publication in June 2020, the article has been viewed 16,339 times, with half the traffic generated in the second half of 2020. In addition, it was picked up by four media outlets and retweeted 354 times.

The hard-hitting blog asserted that

> ... racism is at last everyone's business, and acting against it is everyone's responsibility.

The pandemic and racism are inextricably linked. Both were considered public issues because both have killed people. In May 2020, a teenager caught on video the murder of George Floyd, an African-American, by a White police officer in Minneapolis. The officer pinned down George Floyd on a sidewalk and pressed his knee into the victim's neck for nine minutes. Uploaded on YouTube, the video triggered the largest wave of protests in American history amid a pandemic. A year later, Derek Chauvin, the police officer, was convicted and sentence of life imprisonment in a highly publicized trial.

Racism is a 'co-factor' for COVID-19 and a key determinant of health, said Fiona Godlee. Ethnic minorities are more likely to get infected and die of COVID-19 due to unequal access to healthcare. What the pandemic has brought to the surface is a 'stress test' for everyone concerned about 'structural racism' in healthcare, wrote Christine Douglass, Molly Fyfe and Amali U. Lokugamage in a separate blog for the *BMJ* in June 2020.

According to the Aspen Institute, 'structural racism' and its synonym 'systemic racism' are embedded in America's social, economic and political institutions. Practices, norms, beliefs, policies and cultural representations reinforce racial inequality, most often conferring privilege to 'Whiteness' while simultaneously denying advantages to people of 'colour'. Race often filters policies and practices that range from hiring practices to quality education and healthcare access. Douglass's term 'stress test' is a convenient shortcut for detecting the often hidden and subtle application of race when decisions are made on eligibility for public goods. Put more bluntly, Peggy McIntosh, wrote in her working paper, 'Unpacking the Invisible Knapsack':

> As a white person . . . I had been taught about racism . . . which puts others at a disadvantage, but had been taught not to see one of its corollary aspects, white privilege, which puts me at an advantage . . . white privilege as an invisible package of unearned assets which I can count on cashing in each day, but about which I was 'meant' to remain oblivious.

The cultural representations of racial inequality are even more subtle—the tropes, images, frames and narratives that permeate our language, social media and other forms of communication. Even jokes and seemingly neutral racial slurs are abstruse depictions of people who are not of the White race. They propagate negative stereotypes; unwittingly, they create elusive images and preferences. For example, one might joke about Filipinas' ability to clean an entire household after sex. Although funny and innocent (maybe), these jokes create images and expectations that Filipinas cannot aspire for more than servants with sexual benefits. Or that Korean-Americans will hit the top career ladder only as mom-and-pop grocers, not owners of Carrefour or Tesco. David Benatar calls it 'prejudice in jest'. Check out the expansive database for racial slurs for just about every nationality (even Antarticans were not exempted), ethnic group (Scandinavians, Malayali/Indian), religious communities (Amish, Mormons), and other ambiguous categories (Samis, gypsies). Curiously, there is no category for White Americans.

During the pandemic, hate crimes and violent behaviour towards Asians were observed. 'The haranguing, perorating, bloviating mouth of Donald Trump, who first uttered the phrases 'kung flu' and the 'China virus' in late March 2020 fuelled the hate,' said Representative Ted Lieu of California. To defend his utterances, Trump said:

> It's not racist at all . . . It comes from China. I want to be accurate.

On 16 March 2021, twenty-one-year-old Robert Aaron Long of Woodstock, Georgia, purchased a 9mm handgun at Big Woods Goods. In the early afternoon, he drove up to Young's Asian Massage in Acworth, Cherokee County. He fatally shot two people and wounded three others. Next, Long drove to Piedmont Road in northeast Atlanta to the Gold Massage Spa, less than an hour's drive away, about 48 kilometres from the Young's Asian Massage. There, he killed three women. A Wikipedia entry stated that one of the Gold Spa employees who managed to escape reported that Long said: 'I'm going to kill all the Asians.' Then, across the street at the Aromatherapy Spa, Long killed another woman. By the time he was done with his shooting spree later that evening, he had killed eight people and wounded one. Six of them were Asian women of Korean ethnicity. The Voice of America News reported that a White man and a White woman were killed, and the lone survivor was a Hispanic man from Guatemala. The state police caught up with Long some three and a half hours later trying to make his way to Florida. Long was arrested, tried and convicted in July 2021, four months after the shootings. He was found guilty and sentenced to life without parole.

'Words have power,' read the banner headline of the *Independent* covering the story a year later. In 2020, the rise in anti-Asian violence across major cities in the United States rose by a staggering 169 per cent, reported Kimmy Yam of the NBC news. In New York City alone, the increase in one year was 223 per cent. Between March 2020 and February 2021, the Stop Asian American Pacific Islander Forum (AAPI) Hate, a policy research non-profit organization, reported nearly 3,800 incidents within the pandemic year. The majority of these incidents, around 68 per cent, were directed towards Asian women. The attacks ranged from verbal abuse to spitting, slapping and outright violence. For example, a passenger in a New York City subway slashed a Filipino-American male's face in February 2021. He was taken to Bellevue Hospital and received more than 100 stitches on his face.

Anti-Asian sentiment did not begin with the pandemic. Instead, the virus brought long-held, negative, cultural representations of Asians as a general category to the surface. Massive migration from among diverse Asian communities as early as the sixteenth century sparked anti-Asian attitudes and behaviours. Although anti-Asian racism has a long history, its expression resurfaces during times of crisis. Economic downturns and health crises are perfect storms for the re-emergence of racist attitudes that have lain dormant for a while but are easy to reignite when a confluence of factors emerges.

According to Peter Gordon and Juan José Morales of *Americas Quarterly*, Filipino and Chinese sailors arrived in the early sixteenth century when the Manila galleon trade between Mexico and the

Philippines, as the latter was known to be part of the New Spain. The galleon trade known as the '*nao de China*' was a trans-Pacific trade route between Manila and Acapulco and would last some 250 years. This little-known, global trade network would profoundly affect

> . . . the Americas over two centuries, from the currency people used to the porcelain they bought for their homes.

Not only were consumption tastes affected, more importantly, the reshaping of attitudes and perceptions against the Asians who were regarded as threats to the livelihoods of the locals. For example, in 1635, the barbers of Mexico City protested against what they perceived as unfair competition from Chinese barbers. They asked the municipality to intervene by confining the barbers to the city's outskirts and restricting their number. But after three decades, there were still over 100 barbershops operating in Mexico City. Never was an innocent haircut framed in a historically contentious manner.

During the Gold Rush to California, the Chinese workers consisted of fifty-four Chinese who arrived in 1849. As conditions in South East China worsened after the Taiping Rebellion, many Chinese labourers ventured out West. In his book entitled *The Story of California from the Earliest Days to the Present*, Henry Kittredge Norton wrote in 1913 the arrival of the Chinese 'coolie' and their welcome presence in the early days when drudgery work and cheap wages made Chinese labour indispensable. They were not only prospecting for gold, but also served as cooks, laundry workers and servants. But the dreams of sudden wealth vanished as surface claims became exhausted. By 1855, the gold rush ended a mere seven years of wealth accumulation as quickly as it began. The disappointment of gold-seekers and their unfulfilled dreams found a target: the Chinese coolies whom Governor Bigler of California at the time charged as 'avaricious, ignorant of moral obligations, incapable of being assimilated, and dangerous to the public welfare.' Whether cutting hair or panning for gold, outsiders will always find themselves at the receiving end of abuse over someone else's failure.

Filipino seafarers constituted the first wave of migration to Mexico on the Manila–Acapulco run alongside the Chinese. Many of them settled in Louisiana and Baja, California. They came to work the fruit and vegetable farms. In the immediate aftermath of American annexation in 1899, when Spain ceded the Philippines to America for US$20 million, Filipino migration to America proceeded apace. Many went to Hawaii and California in the plantations, whereas others travelled north to Washington state and Alaska as cannery and fish workers. With the passage of the 1934 Tydings-McDuffie Act, the number of Filipino migrants was limited to fifty Filipinos per year. But World War II reopened migration avenues for Filipinos through intermarriage with American soldiers and recruitment into the military. Also, Filipinos obtained education primarily in the health profession, many of whom remained in the United States for an additional two years to pursue educational and professional goals. This second wave coincided with the removal of national-origin quotas in immigration law in 1965. As a result, immigrants increased fivefold between 1960 to 1980, numbering half a million. There are an estimated 2.5 million Filipino migrants across the United States, the third-largest minority group after the Indians and the Chinese. However, most Filipino migrants are concentrated in California and New York states.

The Japanese, on the other hand, were latecomers. They arrived in Hawaii beginning in 1885, fuelled by heavy taxation on Japanese farmers to finance industrialization during the Meiji Restoration in 1868. According to the Library of Congress, more than 400,000 men and women left Japan between 1886 and 1911. The two most popular destinations were the archipelago of Hawaii and America's Pacific coast. They worked as contract labourers on the sugar plantations or as manual labour on the railroads and sawmills in the mainland. Historyplex.com states that the Chinese Exclusion Act of 1882, considered the first US immigration policy based on race, prohibited the entry of Chinese migrants for ten years and was extended indefinitely in 1902. The exclusionary legislation paved the way for Japanese immigrants. With the outbreak of World War II and the bombing of Pearl Harbor in 1942, the Japanese-Americans were targeted. President

Franklin D. Roosevelt issued Executive Order 9066 that authorized
the forced evacuation and detention of Americans with Japanese
ancestry. According to the National Archives, some 120,000 Japanese-
Americans were sent to 'assembly centres'. After being 'tagged', they
were sent to a long-term 'relocation centre', where they stayed until the
end of the war. There were no charges filed against them. They were
moved inland into remote and desolate places like Minidoka, Idaho;
Topaz, Utah; Heart Mountain, Wyoming; Rohwer, Arkansas. There are
many dark episodes in America's history, and the Japanese-American
internment camps are undoubtedly one of them.

Resentment towards Asians was not always consistent or
widespread. Asians were considered hard-working, quiet, resilient,
non-confrontational, docile. They were tagged as the 'model minority'.
Writing for the *National Geographic*, Erin Blakemore argued that the
Asian stereotype of industriousness and politeness was a myth that
was conveniently deployed in America's courtship of Cold War allies
in the 1950s and 1960s. Asian-Americans were upheld as the desirable
minorities and were contrasted with the Latinos and Black Americans
who, Blackmore continued, were a 'threat to White supremacy'. More
pointedly, the model minority myth was mobilized to de-fang the Black
Power movement and divide Asians from Blacks to delegitimize the
Black revolt.

'I surveyed my overseas extended family and came to realize that they
are part of the successful immigrant story, the ones who "flatter (the)
system",' wrote Hua Hsu of the *New Yorker*. My nephews and nieces,
all first-generation Asian-Americans, are a bunch of model Asians,
all born in America, well-educated, competed in the best American
universities and awarded respectable degrees in medicine, engineering,
nursing, psychology and management sciences. I thought of my niece
in Seattle working as a vice-president in a tech company. In her early
forties, her daughter is an Asian-American preparing for a medical
degree, while her late-teener son does the hockey circuit. Two other
Asian-American children take their seats dutifully in predominantly
White classrooms. Their regular Filipino food is a kind of last-ditch
attempt to preserve some of the Asian taste that could easily evaporate

in a Burger King fast-food stall. They comfortably munch on chicken and pork *adobo* and celebrate birthdays with the traditional Filipino-Chinese noodle dish, the ubiquitous *pancit*. I imagine her every morning putting on her smart suit and high heels, gathering her four children into the family van, dropping them off at school. And then her day of managing at the top of a tech company she aims to build, begins.

Another nephew worked for Elon Musk and can tell you plenty about launching satellites into space. Even at the time of the pandemic, he spent his time bi-coastally as he nervously jetted off to Florida for yet another launch. His wife, a Vietnamese-American, completed her residency in cardiology at the frontlines of the pandemic in a Los Angeles hospital. She referred to that time as a kind of 'shock therapy medical education' even as she was applauded for her smartness and her courage.

And still another nephew married to a Thai-American, both nurses in LA, were also at the forefront of the pandemic. They're exhausted, true, but they occasionally escape to Lake Tahoe with their two children. They are the all-around portrayal of the hard-working Asian-American family. And another niece, a neuropsychologist, married to an Iranian-American engineer, works at the Veterans Administration Hospital, dedicated to helping the former combatants with their post-war traumas. She's seen many of these survivors, from the Vietnam War to the Iraq and Afghanistan wars, which happened long before she was born.

All of them have thus far escaped the racial taunts. Perhaps because of their being at the frontlines of the battle against the virus, they are revered and respected. Or as members of a generation steeped in technology, they are a crucial part of building a technological America that will give the country a considerable edge against its global competitors. They are all Asian-Americans who manifest success and uphold the myth of the successfully assimilated migrant.

Yet it's a brittle narrative because non-Whiteness sticks. White immigrants who came to America several hundred years ago didn't have to struggle with that 'minority feeling'. They just became the majority and everyone else was relegated to the status of outsiders.

At a certain point in my life as an immigrant, I was vaguely conscious of being outside the Black/White racial binary but still within a racial category that was not of the majority. A place called 'racial limbo'. I sensed that at times I was admired because I worked hard and quietly, and sometimes reviled because I didn't stay in place. I moved outside the world of 'different' immigrants. I went to White-dominated graduate schools in New York and Boston. I lived in Manhattan, Cambridge and Palo Alto. I smoked, cussed and used lots of slang I wasn't supposed to. So when I decided to move away, I left the binary. No longer a minority, I was freed from the pressure of living the myth and confirming the model. I broke free of the invisible boundaries of race and gender.

But the disease-race connection was always omnipresent among Asian immigrants. Paula Larsson, a doctoral student at the University of Oxford, published a feature article in the Canadian-based digital magazine, the *National Interest*, on racism in Canada towards Chinese migrants. Aping their American cousins, the Canadians labelled Chinese people as

> ... dangerous to the white, living in the most unhealthy conditions with
> a standard of morality immeasurably below ours.

The Canadian Royal Commission established in 1884 produced a report that stated:

> The Chinese quarters are the filthiest and most disgusting places in
> Victoria, overcrowded hotbeds of disease and vice, disseminating fever
> and polluting the air all around.

In 1885, the Canadian government passed the Chinese Immigration Act, closely following the Chinese Exclusion Act of 1882 in the United States.

The fight against racism is equally long and arduous. The online forum Stop AAPI Hate is a digital advocacy platform to report and document racism through social media. Different ethnic groups have mobilized and engaged in collective action throughout the pandemic. 'Stop Asian Hate' banners have proliferated across the American landscape. Erin Blakemore wrote in May 2021 that the civil rights movement that energized the Latino and Black movements in the 1950s and 1960s was also energizing the Asian Americans. Professor Angie Chuang at the University of Colorado called for an end to the Asian stereotype and to

> . . . band together and develop a new Asian American Pacific Islander solidarity that didn't exist before.

The anti-racist struggle is equally urgent within Asia among Asians. Sylvia Ang, a former postdoctoral fellow at the Asia Research Institute in Singapore, wrote about anti-Chinese sentiments in Australia. She questioned similar acts of abuse against Chinese in South Korea where restaurant owners posted signs like 'No Chinese Allowed'. And Japanese Twitter users who posted the hashtag #Chinese don't come to Japan.

Studies on racism, Dr Ang argued, have traditionally focused on White people 'racializing' others. Concentrating only on Whites versus Others ignores racism by Asians and among Asians. Racism in non-White settings has been overlooked in the literature, and there are very few studies that focus on issues of intra-race racism. Think of racial slurs levelled against Filipinos, Chinese, Malaysians, Indians, Japanese—not by Whites—but by Filipinos, Chinese, Malaysians, Indians, Japanese. In short, amongst ourselves. I've heard many distasteful jokes about their habits and proclivities, incapabilities, misfortunes and incompleteness. It's a sad and sometimes spiteful commentary on how we take umbrage at White racism yet forget our racist attitudes towards those whose skin colour is not that different from ours.

Remember the 2004 movie *Crash*? It's a cinematic melting pot of everything that went wrong with all the different races living in Los Angeles. A critique of the movie said it

. . . examines the dangers of bigotry and xenophobia in the lives of
interconnected Angelenos.

Perhaps this pandemic is very much like the movie. It is a rich, though
disturbing, opportunity to investigate and reflect upon the other
unexplored myth:

. . . racism is something only White people do to others or that racism
can only happen between people of different (skin) colours.

If we could debunk all these other expressions of racism, then living
through this pandemic is undoubtedly worth it.

Chapter 18

It's Only the Beginning

On 31 December 2020 my husband and I toasted the arrival of the New Year with a few friends and an elaborate feast of roasted lamb and champagne. The year ended as I envisioned it would: flushed and slightly inebriated but virus-free, surrounded by close friends who were our pandemic family. Shortly after midnight, my sister called from California to announce that her husband, daughter and herself had just tested positive. She sat forward closer to the screen while she read out the results of the medical test. She was shaken.

It was life's cruel joke, I thought. A divine conspiracy to make me atone for some spiritual transgression I might have committed perhaps in a very distant past life. What started as a culinary celebration ended in psycho-physical indigestion.

Life was undoubtedly troublesome for just about everyone in the world. Unless you lived in the Marshall Islands, which reported only four cases and zero deaths, with zero infections in 2021. However, since the pandemic began in March 2020, our lives have been governed by restrictions, vaccinations, on-and-off lockdowns, breakdowns, safety measures, masks, variants, statistics, exhaustion, impatience, resistance.

Just when we thought Delta was the worst it could get, along came Omicron. Life was upended once again when the new variant was discovered in late November 2021 in South Africa. Stock markets went into a tailspin, so did oil prices. Knee-jerk reactions to the new variant closed down borders yet again. In December 2021, Asia would have slowly reopened to international travel until Japan suddenly closed its borders to all foreign visitors for a month. The Philippines suspended reopening to tourism for two weeks and added eight European and seven African countries to its 'red list.' China remained closed to all foreign travel. Thailand, intent on opening the country to international travellers, modified its 'sandbox scheme' several times in a bid to attract foreign tourists on whom the economy depends. The sandbox scheme allowed fully-vaccinated tourists to enter Thailand without quarantine. However, they were initially confined to the resort islands of Phuket and Koh Samui for fourteen days before they could travel freely throughout the country. The Indonesian government reopened Bali after an eighteen-month closure, but the response was tepid. Singapore and Malaysia initiated Vaccinated Travel Lanes to allow the resumption of cross-border traffic between the two countries, with continuous refinements with the onset of Omicron.

Street protests against restrictions on mobility, mandated masks, health passes and mandatory vaccinations erupted in several European countries—all in the name of rejecting what they believe are infringements on their personal freedoms. The Global Protest Tracker, an initiative of the Carnegie Endowment for Peace, reported over 230 anti-government protests worldwide. Not all were directly related to the pandemic. However, a significant number regarded the coronavirus as a trigger, including budgetary insufficiencies in Guatemala, anti-corruption protests in Cyprus, or prison-sanitation measures in Bolivia. In short, the pandemic ignited collective action the world over.

Bill Gates, valued at US$138 billion, lamented his own challenging year. He divorced his wife of twenty-seven years, his world shrank when his three children left home. Solitary walks in his 66,000-square-foot lakefront home dubbed the Xanadu comforted him. He reported spending more time alone than he ever did; an occasional video bridge game punctuated his lonely days and nights. So yes, one of the wealthiest men on the planet was not exempted from the awful year that was 2021. The year-end issue of *The Economist* called the new normal the 'era of predictable unpredictability'. And that's putting it mildly.

However, to end this year, and this book, on a desolate note, would be unfair, if not outright inaccurate. Difficult as the year may have been, 2021 was nothing like 2020, even if many of the events seemed like a long continuation of what began the year before.

To move forward, we look back to what was a very eventful year in numerous ways.

Today, the world is far ahead in managing the pandemic since the outbreak in Wuhan in January 2020. The website, *Our World in Data*, mentions several staggering positive developments as 2021 heads to a close:

- 55.5 per cent of the world population has received at least one dose of the COVID-19 vaccine;
- 8.35 billion doses have been administered globally;
- 30.58 million are administered daily;
- Five countries have fully vaccinated over 80 per cent of their populations. These are the United Arab Emirates, Cuba, Portugal, Chile and Singapore. If taking into account populations that have received at least one dose, the UAE is at 98 per cent coverage and Cuba at 90 per cent;
- Merck Laboratories has produced 10 million oral anti-viral COVID-19 medicine and expects an additional 20 million courses in 2022. According to Bloomberg, it is packaged under the name Molnupiravir and has already received clearance for use in the UK. Similarly, Pfizer has developed Paxlovid, which will produce 180,000 packs by the end of 2021 and add 50 million in 2022. Both drugs are being touted as potential game-changers. They are intended for home use to prevent hospitalization if taken at the early onset of the virus. They have no known side effects;

- Singapore has developed a saliva-based COVID-19 Antigen Rapid Test to detect infection within 15 minutes with 97 per cent accuracy. Dr Danny Jian Hang Tng of the department of infectious diseases at Singapore General Hospital said that the new test is 'reliable, painless, affordable and convenient.' In addition, this new development expands testing capabilities— another weapon in the pandemic-combatting arsenal.

In Singapore, where I live, management of the pandemic has been an exercise in vigilance. The government has provided daily updates for the past twenty months. Information was vital to contain the viral spread successfully despite numerous inconveniences. There were perennial closures of bars and restaurants. Dining-out regulations fluctuated between two and five people per restaurant table. Planning lunch outings with my girlfriends was continuously rescheduled for months. Then, in early December, we finally met, a planned event meant for June–a six month delay in female bonding.

But so what?

Grumbling, notwithstanding, the citizenry by and large complied. Some found humour in these 'policy yo-yos', as the locals called them. As with the closure of the KTVs (Karaoke TV lounges), a spike in cases in mid-2021 was attributed to 'horny uncles' who frequented these places for their much-needed respite from lockdown and isolation. Likewise, the KTV spread was traced to several Vietnamese hostesses in these lounges. KTVs were humorously dubbed 'Kiss the Vietnamese'.

However, even with the uptick in cases that caused closures, hospitals were never overwhelmed, and there were always sufficient ICU beds to accommodate those who were seriously sick. Death rates remained low; recovery rates are at 97 per cent. Vaccination rates were among the highest globally at 87 per cent completed vaccination by the end of 2021. Masks remained mandatory; they have become part and parcel of our daily wear. The shift from 'pandemic to endemic', which the government announced in July 2021 was a successful storyline: opening up gradually and keep safety measures in place.

Cathy, my hairdresser, mouthed it like a mantra, ready to comply with the regulations to keep her business afloat and her customers safe and confident.

2021 was a year that very slowly ushered in a period of recovery. At times we felt minute signs of progress being swept away by a new mutant. Numbers came down only to climb back up again. But the emergency that was 2020, when the world floundered under the viral assault, felt over. The world was no longer flailing. Science has reconquered the territory of policy and decision-making. Faith in empirical data, despite lingering resistances, was restored. If the number of global vaccines (8.52 billion as of December 2021) is an indicator, the technicians and the scientists have defeated the cynics.

Let us look back so we can look ahead, to help us chart a forward path based on our mistakes and our shortcomings. But, more importantly, let's review our attempts at continuous readjustment and the innovations that this pandemic spawned. We highlight these works-in-progress as though they were flickering footlights on a rocky garden path.

Over the two years, here are a few adaptations: the digital shift; space redesign; juggling work-life balance; remote-work incorporated as daily routine; birthing new/different creativities; virtual celebrations; forging new online communities; knowledge explosion on the Internet.

My life-changing pandemic moment was my entrance into the digital classroom during the Fall and Spring semesters of 2020–21. I conducted classes via Zoom as a visiting associate professor at New York University, Abu Dhabi. In the beginning, I was petrified. Seeing my students' faces on a computer monitor terrified me. It resembled visiting an online doctor or going to an electronic vigil for a departed friend. They were all disembodied, and so was I.

Some forty students who were literally all over the place logged in dutifully twice weekly. One introduced herself from Washington DC Dulles airport on the opening day of classes, fully masked and about to board her plane to Croatia, where she would spend her first semester. Another left mid-semester from Abu Dhabi to Berlin to intern with an NGO for refugee assistance while continuing his undergraduate studies. Two students in the US, one in New Jersey and the other in Colorado, logged in in the middle of the night to make it to my late afternoon class in Abu Dhabi while it was early evening in Singapore. From Sulawesi in Indonesia, a female freshman student missed campus life achingly. Still, she pushed her way into virtual college, determined to land in Abu Dhabi for the second semester after she had received her vaccinations. We often heard the monsoon rains in Indonesia pelting the roof of her home and the charming rooster cackling in the background. Undeterred, she continued her presentation of a case study on Laos hydropower and raised questions about the gendered nature of the public-policy process.

Technology unified our globally dispersed classroom. Our collective commitment to learning went over and beyond the discomfort of different time zones and clunky technologies. Here were a bunch of global kids who made the world their home. And no virus was going to stop them from learning all they could about social research and public policy even if an invisible virus turned their student life upside down.

I travelled the length and breadth of two bedrooms, one of which was my study some ten paces away. Initially, I fumbled in the digital classroom, as did most of us who were suddenly confronted with a technology-driven teaching environment. Pressing the wrong button would make the classroom momentarily disappear and I would silently howl in a panic. A Filipino technician in Abu Dhabi was on stand-by to support me remotely whenever I entered a wrong command on my laptop. I mused that playing golf must have been easier than learning to navigate this digital obstacle course.

Then I realized how human beings are genuinely malleable. By early 2021, when the second semester came around, and I was back in the virtual classroom, the discomfort of Zoom teaching all but evaporated. My reading list was on a virtual bookshelf for my students to retrieve. The course syllabus was successfully uploaded without incident. Students turned in their assignments on the appointed time and date, filed under the proper tabs. My Filipino tech support no longer had to babysit me digitally.

I attended virtual meetings galore: with women writers during our weekly writing workshops; with search-committee members as we listened to candidates competing for the position of dean of the social sciences; with graduating students presenting their year-end capstone (thesis) reports; with faculty from other NYU campuses in Shanghai and New York; with our provost and vice-president conferring the academic degrees to our graduating students virtually. Separated physically but connected digitally, ours was a global community of knowledge seekers. We trusted and respected enough to know that we were a resource to each other, because our experience and commitment to education are the greatest and only assets we had during this utterly precarious time.

I sorely missed my students despite not having seen them corporeally. Many of them have gone out into the real world to take up graduate school, accept jobs as interns or as entry-level policy analysts. One will tackle the painful reality of gender violence in Pakistan and propose policy solutions to end this scourge against women. Others spend semesters abroad travelling to places that excite their curiosity and imagination. I have written numerous recommendation letters, all tailored and customized to reflect their strengths that could change the world.

A year has passed since my odyssey into the virtual classroom, a year etched firmly in my memory. I might even consider the year of Zoom teaching as the single most spectacular event that reshaped my life and my vision of the future. Education happened right in my study room, ten paces away from my living room. Education, as I had always known it for thirty years, was irretrievably transformed. If there was one positive outcome of this pandemic, it was the realization of the immense potential of digital education despite the limitations of not seeing your students, missing out on the close-up processes that indicate to me, their teacher, how I help shaped their perspectives and personal philosophies even in a small way.

But let's look further back beyond this past year, this past century, into many centuries before this one.

I have a historical-sociological view of human life. Thus, I often refer to Fernand Braudel's *longue duree*—the long duration of human life that reveals the underlying structure of societies long ago, beneath the events, beneath the strict facts.

Michael Goodyear's *When Death Docked in Constantinople* is a medieval story of the grandeur of Constantinople (present-day Istanbul), the imperial capital of the Byzantine Empire that was ravaged by four waves of the bubonic plague. In the fourteenth century, Constantinople was a dense harbour city, a site for global trade that connected Asia, Europe and Africa, the perfect gateway for the flow of goods and people across the three continents. Unfortunately, it was also the ideal breeding ground for disease. Goodyear's article described the stench of death across the city in 1347. The bells that pealed from the towering Byzantine churches fell silent, and the streets lay empty. Recall the image of the Duomo cathedral in Milan on Easter Sunday 12 April 2020, some seven hundred years later. The empty cathedral and the barren streets of Milan were an image of desolation. Only Andrea Bocelli's operatic voice broke the stillness.

From Constantinople, the disease spread quickly via trade ships to the rest of Europe. Genoese merchant ships entered Italy from Crimea, bringing the flea that nestled in the backs of black rats carrying the bacteria *Yersinia pestis*. The bacteria attached itself to the human skin, and the scourge began.

Lawrence Wright of the *New Yorker* reviewed the events of the Black Death in Europe in conversation with Dr Gianna Pomata, a retired professor from the Institute of the History of Medicine at John Hopkins University. They retraced the arrival of the plague in Italy. In 1347, twelve ships docked at the port of Messina in Sicily that carried the *Yersinia pestis*, tucked in between the fold of grains and goods that the black rats feasted on. Dr Pomata estimated that the city of Bologna lost half of its population in 1348. Between 1347 and 1351, as the disease spread across Europe, the plague is estimated to have killed 25 million people, equivalent to almost a third of Europe's population at the time.

The pandemic, Lawrence Wright continued, is like

. . . an X-ray of society, allowing us to see all the broken places.

Frank Snowden's recent book, *Epidemics and Society*, echoed the same theme. Pandemics expose underlying social structures, divisions, flaws and fissures. They reshaped human societies throughout the ages. Pandemics forced societies to seek and establish new equilibria because the old pillars that held society together have been eroded and decimated. In numerous ways, pandemic behaviours of the present echo those of the past and how history mirrors all that humans have done and continue to do.

Looking back at who we were, perhaps, we might be guided today to who we might still become. And come to realize, as Dr Pomata put it, the 'extreme fragility of life' and the utter frailty of many of our pursuits.

The pandemic exposed global inequality as one significant facet of our moral relationship to one another. We have long known of this unfortunate global situation, thanks to the works of scholars like Thomas Piketty and Joseph Stiglitz. Yet, it took a virus for us to look more earnestly into the mirror. For two years, we witnessed the ravages of the pandemic in poverty-stricken communities. The poor bore the brunt of the disease, as they always do at any point in history. Channel News Asia in Singapore reported 4 million people were pushed into poverty in the Philippines. Stringent lockdown measures affected incomes and jobs. As a result, its economy contracted by nearly 10 per cent in 2020. The poverty threshold for a family of five dipped to approximately US$240 per month in the first six months of 2021. Already one of the hardest-hit economies in South East Asia, the Philippines reported 2.85 million cases and over 50,000 deaths at the end of 2021. Perhaps not as staggering as the 84 million people living in extreme poverty in India as of May 2021. Yet, a visit to Manila during the pandemic showed the stark face of poverty. Upon exiting the airport, barefoot children descended on our vehicle, tapping the car's window, pleading with me to buy wilted garlands of jasmine flowers for a measly US$0.50, which they would quarrel over when the purchase was swiftly transacted in the moving traffic.

While the poor stayed in place, the rich escaped the dense urban cities, fleeing from the scourge of the viral spread. The medieval scholar, Dr Kathryn McKinley at the University of Maryland, described the similarities of the behaviour of the rich during the bubonic plague and today's pandemic. Then, the poor were packed into tiny apartments and compelled to show up at work.

Italian author Giovanni Boccaccio wrote *The Decameron*, a collection of 100 short stories set during the bubonic plague in Italy. Written in 1351, *The Decameron* chronicled the stories of ten nobles who

> . . . fled the pallor of death hanging over Florence to luxuriate in amply stocked country mansions.

The wealthy closeted themselves in pastoral second homes, similar to American behaviour during the current pandemic. Bloomberg City Lab reported mass migration to more remote suburban areas within two years. The pandemic compressed into months what might have taken years, reported Richard Florida, contributor to the CityLab.

In Medieval Europe, a highly unequal feudal system prevailed. In connivance with church leaders, the king and the feudal lord exercised superior power and control over the serfs and peasants. Together, they formed the apex of a feudal system, and their authority was absolute. At the lowest rung of this pyramidal structure were those who toiled the land, receiving little reward for a lifetime of labour in exchange for food, shelter and protection. The Middle Ages was referred to as the 'era of hardships'. Thus, when the Black Plague struck, mostly the poor suffered from hunger, disease, and ultimately death.

And then there was, of course, antisemitism. Simon Schama, the venerable scholar of Jewish history, wrote in the *Financial Times* in April 2020:

> If scapegoating was always going to be a predictable response of plague-beleaguered powers, the inevitable target of blame was the Jews. At the time of the Black Death, they were accused of poisoning wells in some

places; in others, it was said that they had introduced the disease out of sheer malevolence towards Christians.

During this pandemic, the Chinese bore the brunt. All Asians whom non-Asians can't tell apart ('they all look the same') were victimized, sometimes violently. A sixty-seven-year-old Filipina woman was attacked in Yonkers, New York State in March 2022. A Singaporean student was brutally attacked in London, racial epithets hurled at him. A Chinese teashop owner in Washington DC was pepper-sprayed. Korean women in two Atlanta massage spas were gunned down. The list goes on.

'The swell of xenophobia is unmooring,' wrote the *New York Times* in April 2021. The article concluded that the essence of an individual has all but disappeared, reduced to ethnic stereotyping, racially pigeonholed, collapsing all sloe-eyed men and women as virus-carriers from Wuhan.

'Throughout history, racial and economic inequality went hand-in-hand. A pandemic uncovered these twin scourges, full force. But, while it exposed society's fault lines, these crises also tended to bring profound social change, for good or ill,' wrote Lawrence Wright of the *New Yorker*. The plague ended the Middle Ages, but it also marked the beginning of something grandiose—the Renaissance. Dr Pomata's continuing digital dialogue with Lawrence Wright illuminated this wondrous period of revival in Europe:

> What happens after the Black Death, it's like a wind—fresh air coming in, the fresh air of common sense. Because of danger, there's this wonderful human response, which is to think in a new way. For instance (during the Black Plague), they created boards of health, which are in charge of quarantine. For the first time, hospitals split patients up into specific wards, so that broken bones and wounds, say, were treated separately from diseases. There was also a rise in trade associations, to take care of medical costs and funeral expenses. So, you can see both trends. On the one hand, the plague works as a kind of acid. On the other hand, people try to re-create ties—and, perhaps, better ties. The pandemic

acted as an accelerator of mental renewal. We listen more, perhaps. We're more ready to talk to one another. The atmosphere feels scrubbed clean; the stars are sharper and more visible. The relationship between humanity and the natural world is more balanced and harmonious. Such ecological restorations, of course, have come at the cost of collapsed economies and punctured dreams. Traffic will necessarily resume, oil will be pumped, airplanes will take off. But I wonder if the glorious experience of living with less pollution, however momentary, will linger in our consciousness as an achievable destiny—and as a reminder that major transformations are possible.

Artistry pushed boundaries in Europe's Catholic countries. In Chapter 3 of his book *Epidemics and Society*, Snowden wrote that the plague in Europe during the Middle Ages profoundly affected the arts and culture. The genre of plague literature arose, best exemplified by the works of Giovanni Boccaccio, Daniel Defoe, Alessandro Manzoni, and Albert Camus. In the realm of theatre, Snowden referred to the Oberammergau in Bavaria Germany where the performance of passion plays continued since it was first staged in 1634. The city council took a vow that the people of the town will perform the passion play if they were spared from the Black Death. The play has been staged every year from 1634-1680 and every ten years since.

Because of the problems of mortality and sudden death, the plague provided a moment of transformation in the iconography of European art. Art not only survived but flourished during the plague. The *Guardian* ran a story in March 2020 that Michelangelo and Rembrandt painted their masterpieces in the shadow of the pestilence. Tintoretto, the Italian painter, produced his sixteenth-century masterpiece through a large number of creations for the walls and ceiling of the Scuola Grande di San Rocco in Venice. Paintings portrayed the seemingly random destruction of the plague and the empathy and care aroused in human beings in the face of death. The painter's brush captured the unknowable and the affable, the terrifying and the evocative.

When the plague closed down theatres in England, Shakespeare wrote *King Lear*, *Anthony and Cleopatra* and *Macbeth* in 1606, wrote

Heather O'Neill. Shakespeare was forty-two years old then, having survived four waves of the plague in 1582, 1592, 1606 and 1607. His works punctured and penetrated the

> ... deepest realms of paranoid human solitude.

In the age of coronavirus, India's folk-art scene blossomed. For example, the *Outlook Traveller* reported in July 2020 how Swarna Chitrakar, a housewife in Pingla, a remote village in West Bengal, painted scrolls at the start of the pandemic to illustrate several safety measures during the pandemic. These scrolls depicted in flashing colour the need to cooperate with doctors and nurses, practise social-distancing, and arrest the viral spread. Other Indian artists like Ambika Devi illustrated rural life in India as was her traditional craft with masks and hand-sanitizers integrated in her creations.

But art also delivered us from the doldrums of isolation through irreverent humour. Like the Marsh family of six living in Kent, England. Their pandemic rendition of *Les Misérables* 'One Day More' went viral with over 6 million viewers. The backdrop of brown curtains, dim lighting and amateur musical gadgetry added to the charm. That was in March 2020 while England was under lockdown. Naty R, a commenter on YouTube, wrote:

> Do I change my underwear is a shared worldwide dilemma . . .

elicited hundred more humorous responses online. The original phrasing would have Baron Sacha Cohen, Hugh Jackson and Russell Crowe singing their rage over an impending revolution, as adapted from Victor Hugo's 1862 by the same title. Over eighteen months, the family continuously regaled the global YouTube audiences through their musical parodies.

And then there's Chris Mann, nose and lips stuck on the inside of his picture window somewhere in his England home. His parody of Adele's 'Hello' (topped the record charts in thirty-six countries when it was released in October 2015) garnered over 15,000 comments. A good sampling goes:

'I love these corona songs. People get so creative when they start losing their mind.'

'What have I accomplished? I painted some rocks and organized my soup cans alphabetically.'

'In twenty years, this will be an important historical document.'

Reading the year-end GatesNotes that Bill Gates posted in late 2021, I am struck by what I regard as his 'blueprint for hope'—a four-themed agenda that outlined the post-pandemic period's contours. He's convinced that there is so much potential when the world enters the recovery period in the coming year.

Climate change, he argued, is now a shared global concern, notwithstanding the absences of China and Russia in the COP 26 held in Glasgow in October–November 2021. Over 200 countries attended this event, which included industry leaders, philanthropists and engaged citizens. All of them had the singular goal of avoiding a climate disaster—in and of itself, another kind of pandemic that will most definitely affect all of humanity. Dedicated to cutting methane emissions by 2 per cent and ending deforestation by the end of the decade, COP 26 forged a global coalition to ensure that progress without destroying the environment is achievable.

The digital sphere accelerated during the pandemic. The fastest and more numerous innovations will occur in real-time in this realm. The proliferation of connectivity tools keeps us bound together more tightly through the click of a button, even while the virus keeps us physically separated. I 'saw' my family weekly over Zoom for two years, more than I had ever seen them before the pandemic. It wasn't always a rosy picture of consensuality, but we developed a healthy tolerance and respect for our differences. At the very worst, we submerged the deep-seated disagreements because, in the face of it, holding the family together was far more important than letting our conflicts destroy us.

Third, the health sciences will ramp up as well. Teleconsults will not replace in-person visits to your GP, but there will be a balance between the two modes of medical consultation. Therapy consultations can be done via the digital couch, so there's no need to rush to your counselling session during lunch break. Your doctor could remotely test your blood pressure or through readings from your smartwatch. COVID-prevention and treatment drugs will continue to be refined, and so will preventative drugs against HIV. According to Wikipedia, substantial progress has been achieved with developing a malaria vaccine known as RTS,S/AS01 in October 2021, with a 77 per cent efficacy rate. The latter is a sterling achievement, considering the five decades of research effort that has been put into its development.

Finally, Gates predicted that the acute phase of the pandemic will come to a close in 2022. The coronavirus will not be eliminated. However, Gates believes that the world is better prepared to tackle potentially destructive variants than at any other point in the pandemic so far. These scientific advances will spur further investments in health research and development thanks to genome sequencing capabilities, specifically in South Africa that caught the Omicron variant. One can only hope.

It is tempting to counter optimism. After all, two years have shown us how the world can be turned upside down in a matter of hours. Alex Kliment, Carlos Santamaria and Willis Sparks who write for *Signal*, the GZERO newsletter, offer a chilling prospect for 2022: rising prices due to increasing inflation rates; ransomware attacks occurring every eleven seconds in 2021, accelerating in 2022. Not to mention increasing polarization in political life and the prospect of a long COVID as vaccine maldistribution exacerbates the pandemic rather than ameliorates it. They concluded that the pandemic is far from over—a dissenting voice to Bill Gates's optimism. Plus, creeping surveillance that threatens to erode the boundary between the public and the private, rendering our lives exposed to as-of-yet unregulated technology.

However we may wish to view this period, we cannot afford apathy or complacency. Like Robert Lamm, famed songwriter and founder of the rock-jazz band Chicago, and the song 'Everything is Gonna Work out Fine' that he co-wrote with Jim Peterik under quarantine, I prefer to listen to their plea:

Little by little,
piece by piece,
just find the sweetness
and you will find release.
Little by little,
bit by bit,
meet me in the middle,
and we'll make sense of it.

Robert Lamm's prophetic lyrics will come to pass only in the face of a determined collective effort to eliminate the extremes and close the abyss.

Epilogue

The World at High Noon

'The psychic unity of mankind,' in my view, is the most haunting but also the most beautiful statement in the social sciences. Adolf Bastien, the German ethnographer, surgeon and polymath, developed the concept after extensive travels as a ship doctor all over the world in the late nineteenth century. After completing his travels throughout South East Asia, he produced six volumes of deep ethnography. In these studies, he proposed that all of humanity shared the same mental framework despite the variety of cultural expressions among the peoples he visited.

His plea for universality couldn't be more urgent today in the face of a pandemic that has touched virtually every facet of human life. If Bill Gates is correct, the global health crisis may cease in its urgency and be reduced to a scheduled trip to the GP for vaccinations. But our collective experience with this virus will remain the most significant event that has galvanized global efforts to mitigate, if not outright eliminate, the deleterious effects of the pandemic. We all agree that a return to pre-pandemic life is no longer possible.

Bastien developed his concept in the late nineteenth century, but the strength of the idea endures into the twenty-first, both as a matter of intense debate and disagreement (are we all the same?) and as a shared value (we all stand equal beneath the sun). Bastien, now deceased for a hundred years, haunted us with these questions as we grapple with the variety of conflicts that have swirled around us these past decades. The answer to these questions is not complicated. Yes, of course, we all stand equal beneath the sun.

At the other side of the world and some three hundred years later after Bastien proposed the psychic unity of humankind is Yahya Cholil Staquf, secretary-general of the Nahdlatul Ulama (NU), the world's largest Muslim civil society organization with more than 60 million followers in Indonesia. Pak Yahya, as he is popularly known, founded the global movement Humanitarian Islam. Pak Yahya is a religious leader and a distinguished Muslim scholar who seeks to reform Islam by eliminating what he views as 'obsolete tenets of Islamic orthodoxy that enjoin religious hatred, supremacy and violence.' He seeks to restore

. . . *rahmah* (universal love and compassion) to its rightful place as the primary message of Islam.

Speaking via Zoom at the United Nations Panel in September 2020, Pak Yahya reiterated

> . . . the message of Islam was delivered by the Prophet Muhammed for the sole purpose of inculcating noble character, and thereby perfecting the moral framework of humanity. The primary message of Islam is *rahmah*, or universal love and compassion [as stated in Qur'an 21:107]. As we can see from this message, the fundamental aspiration of Islam is in full alignment with that of the Universal Declaration of Human Rights.

He delivered the same message to 800 Jews, Muslims and Christians on a visit to Jerusalem in June 2018 on the occasion of Eid-al-Fitr, the holiday marking the end of Ramadan, the Muslim month of fasting. At the Tower of David Museum, Pak Yahya joined the crowd with Brother Franz von Sales and Rabbi Yakov Nagen in an interfaith 'singalong' to the tune of Bob Marley's 'One Love,' in three-part harmony and three languages: English, Hebrew and Arabic.

Pak Yahya stands at the helm of two institutional initiatives: the Institute for Humanitarian Islam and the Center for Shared Civilizational Values. Both these organizations are dedicated to lofty goals: to stop the political weaponization of identity, curtail the spread of communal hatred and foster the emergence of a truly just and harmonious world order founded on the values of solidarity and respect among diverse peoples, cultures and nations of the world.

Pope Francis, leader of the 1.2-billion-strong Catholic church, is without question a global leader. He is dedicated to the upliftment of all humankind regardless of faith. In late 2021, Francis called upon world leaders to address the climate crisis and the need for 'radical decisions'.

Jorge Mario Bergoglio, the former Archbishop of Buenos Aires, Argentina, was elected Pope in March 2013 and became the Roman Catholic Church's 266th pope. Always dedicated to the poor and cognizant of the significance of the platform of the papacy, Francis very early on announced his openness and inclusivity. Valeria Bellagamba, associate dean for academic and global operations of Georgetown University's McDonough School of Business, said that Francis has

> . . . taken a unique stance in the rejection of the norm . . . He declared that God redeemed all of us, not just the Catholics. He is there for everybody.

In 2015, Francis issued the *laudato si*, the 'ecological encyclical', and a concrete programme of action for human development founded on the principles of inclusivity, climate justice, global justice and ethical investment. Echoing the message of Adolf Bastien, Pope Francis issued a message during COP 26 that called for

> . . . a recognition of the unity of our human family in God's plan for the world.

Adolf Bastien developed his thesis in the context of aggressive colonialism, a period in human history when European countries and America vied for domination and control of overseas territories. The underlying discourse of European colonialism was 'mission civilisatrice', the civilizing mission, to promote the cultural assimilation of the non-White Other (the 'primitives'). In comparison, Pak Yahya and Pope Francis promote humanitarian Islam and the synodality in the context of a highly toxic geopolitical environment. Before the pandemic, geopolitical rivalries have been marked by what James M. Dorsey terms 'civilizational politics'. Dorsey argued that world leaders, conservative and far-right politicians and activists frame the emerging geopolitical rivalry as the rise of 'civilizationalism'. Its political handmaiden, guardian and custodian is the civilizational state whose legitimacy rests on a distinct civilization rather than on the nation state's concept of internationally recognized borders, territorial integrity, language and citizenry.

Today, the new world order arising out of civilizational politics is being shaped by what the anthropologist, Clifford Geertz, terms 'primordial identities'—those of racial, ethnic, religious affiliations—that hark back to earlier centuries of civilizational order.

Central to civilizational politics is the weaponization of religion and race. The propagation of *absolute truths* is evident in various religions and has resonance in many countries worldwide. Using religion as a social and political weapon promotes ethnic and religion-based ultra-conservatism and/or hyper-nationalism. This trend has been on the rise in recent years and has seeped into the politics of various countries, although its antecedents date further back in history. A *New York Times* op-ed by Amy Sullivan in December 2017 dubbed it 'Fox Evangelicalism'—a specific strain in American Evangelism that constitutes an emerging worldview characterized as 'nationalistic, race-baiting, fear-mongering politics'. Buddhist nationalism has fuelled hatred against Rohingya Muslims in Rakhine State in South East Asia. Since political liberalization in 2012, Myanmar has witnessed the emergence of deep-seated grievances against Muslims in the country, who constitute a minority of some 1 million amidst 53 million. The use of religion has been central to the campaign to expel the Rohingya and cleanse Rakhine State by the Burmese military, who view them as migrant workers from the British colonial era and therefore are outsiders. Many examples across the globe exemplify this growing trend. Contemporary reform movements such as those promoted by Pak Yahya and humanitarian Islam and Pope Francis's 'laudato si' are vital for ethnic, religious and civilizational pluralism.

Writing over one hundred years apart, reared in different intellectual traditions and distant geographies, separated only by circumstance, Bastien, Staquf and Pope Francis remain united in their shared vision of humanity. The political project of this era is, undoubtedly, democracy—a global political project that will arrest the rollback of democratic practices, strengthen it further and promote a world order founded on principles and practices of stakeholder dialogue. Much like Pope Francis's synodality—an effort at a global conversation among all the faithful, not just among the hierarchy of bishops and archbishops— to inform the pope of the direction of the Catholic church in an era of strife, division and discord.

The swirl of human events these past several decades has brought into sharp relief the civilizational problematic that constitutes the foremost humanistic challenge of our time. While the undercurrent of simmering conflicts exists among these powers, can new geopolitics provide opportunities for re-fashioning a more just and balanced world? Are there prospects for cooperation among global authorities in an emerging multipolar world with no clear hegemon? How can emerging powers behave like 'global stakeholders' and create a new world order premised on joint responsibility and collective undertaking?

We are at high noon. The global climate crisis threatens our survival as a species. Our multilateral institutions are being severely tested to contain potential flashpoints from the Crimean Peninsula to the South China Sea. Populist politicians threaten democracies around the world. These authoritarian populists prey on the fears and insecurities of citizens and promise quick fixes while stoking anger and resentment. Incivility in global public discourse has also become a new normal. Four-letter words have become fashionable. Into the third year of the pandemic, there is a consensus that disruptions in all facets of our lives will continue.

We could indulge ourselves in a global sulk, groan about our exhaustion, bemoan the normalcy that we once craved for, never to return. Spend our lives in a permanent grump.

Or we can grasp this moment, no doubt a long one, instead, to revel in this momentary stillness and enjoy the sparks that may come when we stand in the centre of our enforced silences. The astrophysicist Paul Sutter of Stony Brook University and Flatiron Institute wrote a blog in April 2020 about Isaac Newtown who fled the Black Plague in London in 1666 to hang out in his mother's farm in Lincolnshire. There, Sutter wrote,

> . . . free from distractions, he made some of his most powerful insights-
> -like his thoughts regarding falling apples.

His thoughts ruminated in the orchard when an apple fell and ignited a spark. And so the theory of gravity was born. Under lockdown.

Or like Damir Marusic and Shahi Hamid, bloggers of the newly launched *Wisdom of the Crowd*, advising us to regain a sense of the possible, re-engage through

> . . . planning and strategizing rather than watching life passively with detached horror—and [in the meantime], to try to be more charitable.

That's excellent advice for those of us who are, in their words,

> . . . crouch[ed] down, trapped in time, mute, helpless.

From the very young and most inspiring poet Amanda Gorman are inspirational verses for the New Year in 2022:

> *What was cursed, we will cure.*
> *What was plagued, we will prove pure.*
> *Where we tend to argue, we will try to agree,*

Those fortunes we forswore, now the future we foresee,
Where we weren't aware, we're now awake;
Those moments we missed
Are now these moments we make,
The moments we meet,
And our hearts, once all together beaten,
Now all together beat.

Come, look up with kindness yet,
For even solace can be sourced from sorrow.
We remember, not just for the sake of yesterday,
But to take on tomorrow.
Come over, join this day just begun.
For wherever we come together,
We will forever overcome.

These past two years felt at many times debilitating and oppressive. Fretting and waiting for my husband to come out of an induced coma in May 2021, I hunkered down with paints, gel pens, markers and brushes to fight off depression. I stared into midnight gardens and mandalas printed on black paper, yearning to explode with colour under the weight of my fingers, deftly manoeuvring the pens and brushes across colourless blackened pages. Right there, I discovered the power of shades, hues, tones and textures. All of these shifted my perception away from bleakness. Colour, ink and texture re-framed my world. My brain formed images of magentas blended with sepia brown, layered with mineral green and a dash of tabasco red to produce a branch of autumn leaves. The multi-coloured images overtook the darkness. Each pen and brushstroke, every shaded petal and layered twig lifted the fog, one heavy cloud at a time.

I dispensed with Christmas shopping in 2021. Instead, I gifted all my siblings with digital presents from my arsenal of a year's artwork. Each of them received a hand-painted rendition of their favourite Psalm prayers encased in wine-red tropical flowers, speckled brown zebras, tangerine carp in electric-blue ponds, triumphant silver angels and their platinum trumpets, mischievous garden elves, jade-green toads, whimsical fairies with lilac faces and purple hair, sparkling mandalas like explosive fireworks splattered across a darkened page. The grip of trauma loosened, and my composure returned. Giving to them, I was giving to myself too.

Acknowledgements

During the difficult period of the pandemic, especially during the lockdowns, many people contributed to the writing of this book. Among them was my mother and her caregivers, who continue to care for my mother under the most stringent circumstances given her fragility and very advanced age. My mother's valiant struggles to stay alive just to see her children is a perennial story; that story shaped the writing of this book. Her will to defy the virus is formidable. My brothers and sisters spread across three continents have been abiding presences throughout this book. Over two years of digitalized family life was tough on everyone, but not once did we falter on our Sunday digital reunions. Their stories interweave with mine, and this book couldn't have been written without the generosity of their sharing.

Friends across the globe read portions of the book while they too struggled with isolation and separation. My gratitude goes to Caroline Brassard, Randy David, Robert Klitgaard, Ronald Llamas, Robert Upton. Dr Eugene Bingwen Fan was my attending physical at Tan Tock Seng Hospital during the period of long confinement. During periods of doubt and uncertainty, he gave me reassurances that I was stronger than the virus. He remains a friend to this day.

My gratitude to James who saw me through the very difficult period of long COVID and shared with me, almost on a daily basis, the physical and emotional toll of the infection. The two years of constant togetherness were the best in our marriage. It is an irony of life that the pandemic has brought us both a deep intimacy and enjoyable togetherness that we might never have achieved if the virus had not arrived in our lives.

Finally, to all the staff of the Tan Tock Seng Hospital, even if I have not had the privilege of knowing them all by name. It is to them that I truly owe the return to the fullness of my life.